A Gang Member's Tale

BY PETER WOLFINGER

A GANG MEMBER'S TALE

Library of Congress Control Number: 2020908900

Printed in the United States

PROJECT MANAGER: Kassandra White
INTERIOR LAYOUT AND JACKET DESIGN: Nicole Sturk

ACKNOWLEDGMENTS

I would like to thank our Lord for allowing me to live long enough to write this story. I'm sure that when I go home, He will give me a bill for a chiropractor, for the many times he carried me throughout my life.

Many thanks to my wife and my friends for their support.

And a very special thanks to my cousin, Audrey, for guidance and support. Audrey is the author of the *Lady's Desire* series, which can be found on Amazon.

Another special thanks to Kassandra White and the team at Atlantic Publishing Group. They believed in my manuscript and helped this dream become a reality.

Last but not least, thanks to life. We do not realize how precious our life is until we are about to lose it.

DISCLAIMER

While actual persons and events, certain characterizations and incidents inspired this story, locations and dialogue were fictionalized.

TABLE OF CONTENTS

A Gang Member's Tale

CHAPTER 1

The year was 1957, and I was 14. That is the year when I had my first encounter with gangs; I would walk past a large apartment house, and a group of boys and girls would hang out in the front of the building, challenging other boys that passed their building to a fight. Their leader's name was Lenny, and he would push you until you both would fight. I would always lose, mainly because he was about three years older than me. Their plan was to force you into the hallway, then into the courtyard of the building. The courtyard was a big square area that separated the apartments, and to the rear of the courtyard there was an alley that led to the boiler room, with no way out except through them. They knew that if they got you cornered, you would have no choice but to fight.

One day, while I was walking pass the apartment buildings, Marylou was standing in the doorway of the apartment building. She held her hand out for me to come to her. Marylou was about two years older than me and very easy on the eyes; with her hand still out she said, "Come with me; I want to show you something." I replied that I knew it was a trick. She laughed and said no as she led me to the boiler room.

Once inside the boiler room, she kissed me and put my hands on her breasts while she unbelted my pants, then she put her arms around my neck and jumped up, wrapping her legs around me. All the while I was thinking, "Don't come." I have to say, I lasted longer than I thought I would. When we finished, she kissed me and said, "You should go before you're seen here."

I fixed my pants, still wondering what had just happened as I opened the boiler room door. I went up the steps into the courtyard, when suddenly, the side door opened, and Lenny came out. Once he saw me, his face turned red with anger, and he charged at me, head down like a bull. His boys followed right behind him.

I met him and got him into a headlock, swinging him to the ground. This was the first time I was on top, and it felt good. I raised my hand to hit him, but something hard hit my head, and everything went black.

When I woke up, I was at the bottom of the alley steps. My head hurt, and I felt light headed. I felt my head, then looked at my hand and saw blood. Looking around, I didn't see anyone, so I headed to the hallway door. Once outside, I looked around; there was no one in sight, and I started for home.

I lived in a small apartment house above my family's Plumbing & Heating store. The store was in front with an apartment in rear, where my Aunt Pat lived; upstairs there were two apartments. The front was where my grandparents lived, and my family lived in the rear.

I went to open our apartment door, but it was locked. I banged on the door, yelling "Mom open up!" When she opened the door, she saw me, screamed, and fainted. My grandfather opened his door to see what the noise was; he looked at my mom lying on the floor, then me. Grabbing me by the arm, he said, "Get in here and sit down." As I sat there, I asked about my mom and who would take care of her. Grandpa replied that I was the first priority; he applied something that burned, then some bandages. Once done, he smacked me in the face. I said, "What was that for?"

He replied, "For not ducking. Now let's take care of your mother."

My mother was lying on the floor, and grandpa gently put a cool rag on her head. As she woke, she asked, "Where's my baby?"

I replied, "Right here," as we helped her up and into a chair. I then told her I fell.

Grandpa said, "Here is the key to the shop. Go down and sort the pieces of pipe into the same size, and don't go to sleep." Our family owned a plumbing and heating company and kept the supplies in the basement of the shop.

I went to the cellar where the pipes were and started to sort them out. I heard my sister and her girlfriends running up the steps to our apartment. Paying no mind, I continued to sort the pipes. Then I heard a voice calling my name, and I replied that I was downstairs in the basement. My sister's girlfriend, Carol, came down the steps and ran over to me saying, "I heard you were hurt," as she reached up, touching my head. Our lips were close, so we kissed, and as I pulled back, she whispered, "I'll jerk you off if it makes you feel better."

"Sure would," I replied, and she giggled as she lifted her blouse, showing me her breasts. I took out my family jewel. She grabbed a hold of it, kissing me while she was jerking me off. Every so often, I was able to feel her breasts. We had just finished when we heard the shop door open, followed by my sister, Joanne, calling for Carol. "I'll be right there," replied Carol. She fixed her blouse, kissed me once more, and ran up the steps. I could hear them talking as they closed the shop door.

I turned back to sorting the pipes and said to myself, "What is happening?" About an hour later the shop door opened again, and I heard my father walking over to his desk. As he sat down, he hollered "Pete, come up."

I sat there looking at him when he said, "Tell me what really happened." I told him everything that happened, leaving out Carol. He sat there for a few moments then said, "Son you are growing into a tall, handsome, young man. You look older than you are. Young girls will be attracted to you. Please be aware, they may have boyfriends, brothers, and fathers that will do you harm if they catch you with their girls. Also, you have to protect yourself; do I have to tell you about the birds and the bees?"

"No," I replied.

He said, "OK, then don't bring home any babies from Britain. Go upstairs and get something to eat."

The next morning, I was sitting in the front of my apartment house when Charlie walked by. I had known Charlie for a while; he lived around the corner, and our mothers shopped at the same stores. Charlie looked at me and said, "What happened to you?" I told him the story; he replied, "That is because you don't belong to a gang. Come with me and join ours. We call our gang the Quantrills."

As we walked past Lenny's apartment house, we saw no one, but Charlie said, "Lenny sees us but doesn't want trouble with our gang." We walked a few more blocks until we came to a group of guys just hanging out on the corner of 118th Street and 101st Avenue. Charlie introduced me to all the members, and they just accepted me.

While hanging out on the corner, we would play handball, cards, sing in a group, and whistle at the girls as they passed by. We all wore motorcycle jackets and the Quantrill medallion around our neck. At night we would sing under the streetlight and share a bottle of beer that the older members bought us.

CHAPTER 2

One day, Willie, the president of our gang, said the Rockaway and Fulton gang was in our territory, so we had to be careful. He no sooner
finished warning us when we heard Charlie screaming. We turn to see
Charlie running toward us with about six guys chasing him. Once they
saw us, they stopped, but only for a few seconds, then they charged us. We
stood our ground and waited. When they got close, we charged them. The
fighting was fierce. Antennas were broken off the cars and used as whips,
but we mainly used our fists, feet, and heads. The fight was turning in our
favor, so the Fulton gang members started to retreat up 118th Street toward Atlantic Avenue with us in hot pursuit. As luck would have it, while
we were running past my church, the religious class was coming out of
church. I could hear them hollering to my sister that they saw me running
by with the gang.

Once we got up to Atlantic Avenue, traffic was very heavy and the Fulton
Street gang was dodging cars to get to the other side of the street. By the
time we got to the other side, they were far away, so we all turned around
and headed back to our corner, laughing and joking and saying who hit
whom and how they ran from us. Most of us had welts on our bodies;
Eddy had a real big cut across his face, either from an antenna or a razor
blade. Fortunately, the cut wasn't that bad, and he didn't have to go to the
hospital.

The next day, as I was returning home for lunch, I saw Reverend Reed
coming out of my father's shop. "Not good," I said to myself. I tried to pass
my father without him seeing me. I didn't make it, and he called me in his
office. As my father started speaking to me, I couldn't tell if he was mad

or not. "Reverend Reed seen me today and suggested that you attend the social meetings your sister goes to. It's Monday, Wednesday, Friday from 6-8, and you're in luck; today is Wednesday."

I replied "OK," and started walking to the door. I heard him say to try to stay out of trouble because school would be starting soon.

As soon as my sister and I walked in the church foyer, I could feel the eyes on me. Reverend Reed introduced me, then we went to the recreation room, and, after a prayer, the reverend said, "I'll leave you to enjoy yourself," then he left.

The girls started playing music and dancing with each other; the boys just stood there watching. I grabbed a girl and started dancing, then each girl wanted a dance. I was really having fun, but the boys started to get mad. However, they were afraid of me, so they started to ask the girls to dance when a slow dance was playing. At the end of the evening, when we started to leave, a very pretty girl named Stacy, came up to me and asked if I would walk her home. My sister had already started for home with her girlfriends, so I said sure. As we started walking, I saw a guy starting to walk toward me out of the corner of my eye, but a few of his friends stopped him.

As we walked to her house, she asked if I had a girlfriend. I replied, "No, do you have a boyfriend?"

She laughed and said, "A few," as she grabbed my hand.

When we got to the front of her house, she turned and kissed me, saying "I hope you will be seeing me more often." Then, she entered her house.

I was walking back to my house when Lester pulled up and asked if I wanted a ride. Laughing, I replied, "Sure, nice ride. How long did you have it?"

"A couple of weeks, been changing plates," replied Lester. As I was getting out, I said, "Les, you should park it and walk away. You had it too long."

As he pulled away, he yelled, "I'll think about it."

The next day I woke up, got dressed, and asked my mom if I could have the empty bottles to turn in for some change. She said that I could, and I took them to Eric's butcher shop and got a dollar. That was good enough for me, so I headed toward 118th Street.

I saw Charlie and asked if there was anything for us to do. Charlie replied, "Yup, we going to pay a surprise visit to Rockaway and Fulton Sunday night. They're having a big dance in a church called Saint Margaret's, so we're going pay them a visit. We're waiting for Will now to tell us more." About an hour later, Will showed up and said, "Let's go over to John's place and discuss our plan."

John opened the door with a wet towel in his hand, and my eyes almost came out of my head. There was a girl about 18 years old on her knees in her panties and bra; she had red welts on her back. John said to the girl, "Go into the bedroom and wait for me." John turned to us and said, "She likes to be hit before we have sex. Everyone find a place to sit, and let's start planning." I was staring at John's hands, which were on the table. One hand had two fingers missing; the other hand had one finger missing. John noticed me staring at his hands. Looking up at me, he said "Wondering how I lost my fingers?" Without waiting for an answer, he started telling how he lost his fingers. The game he explained was very expensive and dangerous; it was called fingers. One hand was tied to a table, fingers spread out. A Zippo is placed in your free hand. Everyone who was playing placed a $100 bill on the table, then with your free hand you flipped the cover of the lighter, struck the lighter, and if it lit, you won the money on the table. If it didn't, you lose the tip of your finger of choice. "Do you want to play?" he asked. I turned down his offer, and John laughed, then we started talking of a plan of attack.

Will said there would be a change in plan because we would be outnumbered. "Maybe if the Cousins join us we may stand a chance. Let's do this; Pete, Charlie, and Eddie will go as our war counselors. The Cousins will send their counsel, and maybe between the two of our gangs, we can make peace with Rockaway and Fulton. You will know the Cousin counselor; he is about an inch taller than you, Pete, and has blonde hair. I will reach out to the Cousins and tell them of our plan." We spent the rest of the night just hanging out.

The next morning, I was getting ready to go out to the corner and hang out when my mother said, "Peter, please come with me to the hospital to see my father."

"Sure no problem, Mom," I said.

As we waited for the bus, my mother started to cry. I put my arm around her and said "Don't worry, he will be OK." When we arrived at Queen General Hospital, my mother and I walked down the narrow hall of the hospital, and we could see the swinging doors leading to the large public ward for the poor. I held the doors open for my mother to pass. When we walked through the doors, we saw her father lying in a bed located in the far corner of the ward. As we approached him, I grabbed her hand and told her to be brave and not to let grandpa see her crying. When we reached his bed, mom bent down, kissed his bald head, and starting talking to him.

Grandpa didn't recognize us at all; he just stared up at the ceiling. Mom started talking to him, and even though he didn't respond, mom kept talking. Looking at him, I couldn't help but remember how at one time he looked so strong and was such a great carpenter and how he would bring pastries to our apartment every Sunday and talk to mom. He didn't say much to me, just hello and how is everything. As mom was talking to him, she noticed that he had dirtied himself. She sent me to find some towels, so we could clean him up. After cleaning him, we shaved him and washed him down again. Just as we were finishing, an aid came by with food and left it on the side of the bed. My mother tried to feed him, but he didn't want to eat and kept looking up at the ceiling. Looking around I noticed a nurse, and I asked if she could help us feed my grandfather. She looked me right in the eye and said, "I'm too busy, and he's dying."

I said, "If you don't help my mother, I'm going to throw your ass out the window." The nurse looked at him, then went over and started helping my mother, but it didn't matter. He wouldn't eat. I looked at my mother; she looked like her heart was breaking. I felt like beating every nurse and doctor that I saw. I felt so helpless, not being able to help my mother. After a while a nurse came over and said we had to leave because visiting hours were over. I had to control the urge to hit the nurse for telling us to leave. My mother said thank you, kissed my grandfather on the head while telling him everything will be alright, and promised she would see him in a couple of days. As we were waiting for the bus, my mother scolded me for what I said to the nurse. She said that I was only 14 and I would understand when I got older. I just looked at her and said, "Yes, mom." But I felt she was wrong; no one should be treated like that. Even though I was 14, I knew deep down that I would not want to die old and alone in a city ward.

Wednesday came fast, and I was anxious to go to the church dance and take up where I'd left off with Stacy. As my sister and I walked into the church, everyone was staring at me, and my sister left my side to join her girlfriends. Rev. Reed said, "Let's go into the rec room."

Once in the rec room, we said our prayers, and the music started. I was walking toward Stacy when Rev. Reed called me over asked to speak to me, in his office. He said, "Please, sit down." Looking at me, he said, "A couple of silver candle holders are missing, and I was told you were the last person to be seen near them." I replied that he was wrong and that I had no idea what he was talking about. I got up and started toward the door. He hollered out, "I'm not accusing you. I'm asking." I didn't look back, I just kept heading to the rec room. Once there, I looked around and saw all the boys standing around laughing and joking, I walked over to them; they stopped and looked at me. I told them that whoever took the candleholders had better put them back tonight; if not I would beat the shit out of everyone one of them. I turned and saw Rev. Reed coming, so I started toward the church doors. He was yelling my name, but I kept walking out.

I started walking to the corner. The guys were there, group singing, playing cards, and talking to each other; they were surprised to see me so early. I explained what had happened, but they just laughed and said to forget about it. I stayed for a few hours, then started for home.

I was passing the shop when my father hollered for me to come in. Sometimes I believed he had eyes behind his head. I sat in the chair and waited for him to complete what he was doing.

He turned toward me and said, "Rev. Reed called and told me what happened, and he wants to apologize to you and would like you to come back; I told him that it is up to you."

I said, "No thank you, Dad."

He smiled and said, "OK no problem. Try to stay out of trouble."

The week flew by, and before we knew it, it was Sunday, and we were standing in front of St. Margret's Rec Hall. I turned to Charlie and Eddy and said, "We'd better take our gang medallions off for our own safety. I'll go look for the guy Tom." They agreed and said they would wait by the front door. The dance floor was crowded with a lot of teenagers dancing, but after a while I spotted a tall guy that fit the description that Will gave. He was dancing with a pretty girl; as I got close, the music stopped, and he walked away toward a group of guys. The music started up again for a slow dance. I asked the girl if she cared to dance; she looked up at me and said yes. We were dancing for a few minutes when I felt a hand on my shoulder, turning me around to face him. I said, "Hi. Tom?"

He said, "She's my girl, and I know who you are. We've been waiting. There will be no peace." Then he gave me a wicked smile. I hit him with an upper cut, sending him into a group of teens dancing. Then I turned to run when I spotted his girl standing there in front of me. I put my arm around her waist and kissed her. She smiled, and I took off running for the front door; as I ran passed Charlie and Eddie, I yelled, "Trap!"

There were about four to six guys chasing me. I had a half a block lead, and they weren't catching up, so after six or seven blocks they gave up. The problem was, I didn't know where I was. I spotted a man walking his dog, and I went over and asked him where the subway was; he pointed and said it was four blocks straight ahead.

The next morning, I got up and headed to the corner to see and tell everyone what happened. When I got there, only Jim, Will, and Tom were there. I told them about the night before, and Will replied, "At least you got away. Charlie was arrested for carrying a knife. Eddie was arrested for carrying a club. I guess we have to keep our eyes open when we are alone."

We started playing cards, and before I knew, it was 10 o'clock in the evening. I started for home, thinking about how much money I won. Before I knew it, I was at my front door. I pushed open the door and felt someone hit me in the chest. I flew out and landed on the ground; I quickly got up, automatically putting my hands up for defense. Tom came out of my hallway with a smile, "Remember me," he asked as he charged me, pinning me up against a parked car. We started hitting each other as his gang circled us, cheering him on. The noise bought down my father, grandfather, and a few neighbors.

My father entered the circle and stopped the fight, asking "What is going on?"

Tom replied, "I have a beef with your son. He hit me and kissed my girl." My father asked if that was true.

I replied, "Yes."

"OK, get away from the cars and store windows." We moved down to the corner of the block. Everyone formed a circle around us. We danced around each other, then started throwing punches at each other. Tom got into me a bear hug, but I hit him in the face with my head, breaking the hold. Then I threw punches, backing him up. We were swinging hard and fast, hitting every-way and everywhere we could. Finally, I hit him, and he went down and didn't get up fast enough. I was on him, trying to pin his arm down, but he was too strong and kept punching me and trying to throw me off him. I grabbed his head and started banging it on the side-walk. My father said, "Stop." A voice from the gang said that it was fair, but my father said, "I don't care. My son can kill him," as he was pulling me off Tom. "Now pick up your friend and leave." After everyone left, I stood there with my father and grandfather, and I started to cry with relief. My father put his hand on my shoulder and said, "It's OK. You did good. Let's go upstairs and get you fixed up. You will be hurting tomorrow."

I woke up around lunchtime, feeling pain all over. I looked in the mirror and scared myself. I had a black eye, bruises, and cuts all over me. As I sat down at the table, my father smiled and said, "I'm proud of you son. That guy was older and bigger than you, and you still won. But next time try not to kiss another guy's girl."

CHAPTER 3

It was the first day of school, which was usually the roughest day for me. I stood in front of the mirror, checking to see if any of the bruises were still there. Luckily, I heal pretty fast. I wasn't looking for trouble, at least not on the first day. I said to my sister, "Joanne, let's go. You don't want to be late your first day of high school."

Joanne said, "Please don't tease me. I scared enough." I told her not to worry and that I was there for her. Then I gave her a hug. When we got to school, I walked her to her homeroom. Then I went to mine.

As I entered my homeroom, the teacher said, "I see, Mr. Wolfinger, you are starting the year off as usual, late. That will be one-day afternoon detention." When the bell rang, I ran to my sister and walked her to the next class. By the end of the day, she knew where all her classes were, and I had eight days detention. As I went to my classes, l noticed a pretty little brunette, and every time I looked at her, she would look back and smile. I made a note of that in the back of my mind. I would have to meet her.

The month went fast, and before I knew it, it was November, and I turned 15. I was behaving pretty well in school. I mean, I had morning detention and afternoon detention, but I had not reached the limit of 20 days because the next step would be suspension. I had more girlfriends than guy friends, and my main problems were not wearing a tie and being late to class. I blame that on Rose; she always wanted sex on the stairwell.

The lunch room had separate eating areas: one for girls and one for boys. We would talk to each other while waiting in line to get our lunch, then go sit at a table. Most of the tables were full, except for ours; at our table there were only three of us: Jack, LeRoy, and myself. One day while I was eating, I noticed a small nerd standing in the center of the room. No one was allowing him to sit at their table, so I yelled at him to come join our table. LeRoy said, "Fuck no," but Jack laughed and said he could come over. He came over, sat down in front of me, and introduced himself to us, and we did the same. His name was Paul. His father was just transferred here, and this was the first public school he ever went to. We all laughed and said welcome.

One day while sitting down to lunch, LeRoy turn to Paul and said, "Give me a quarter."

Paul replied, "I don't have a quarter." LeRoy then told him to just give him what he had. I said, "Don't give him anything."

LeRoy stood up and said, "Then you give me the quarter." I stood up across the table from him and informed him that I was the wrong guy to ask. I grabbed his long, Slim-Jim tie, which hung down to his balls, and jerked him at a 45-degree angle across the table. I grabbed his legs and flipped him on the bench, taking his tie and wrapping the tie around the bench and his neck. I started to choke him; he tried to hit and get free. Jack kept his boys from helping him. A gym teacher grabbed me from behind, and a few other teachers came to help him. The three of us were taken to the principal, Mrs. Koch.

She looked up and said, "Why is it always the same three troublemakers? OK, who started the trouble?" We all pointed to the teacher, but she didn't think that was funny and assigned us three weeks dry lunch. (This was a classroom where you bring your lunch and drink, and if you didn't bring a drink, you could not get a drink of water. There was no talking allowed, and they would put the meanest teacher in the room to make sure the rules were enforced.)

As we were going back to our class, I said LeRoy, "Why are you mad? I was helping you turn into a white man."

LeRoy replied, "Fuck you. Why'd you stick up for him?"

I replied, "One, he was sitting with us, meaning he was one of us. Two, he's very smart. I saw him in my sister's class, and we may need him for homework or a report. Three, you're a bully; you pick on easy targets. Notice you didn't ask the jocks for money because they'd have kicked the shit out of you. Now are we all friends?" The three of us shook hands and headed for our class.

A few days later I was walking in the hall to meet my sister when a jock walked past my sister. He hit her books out of her hand and kept walking, laughing. My sister just bent down and started to pick up her books. I ran and caught up to him, pushing him forward, but not hard enough to hit the ground. He turned and said, "What's the big idea?"

I replied, "Go back and help my sister pickup her papers and books."

He laughed and said, "Make me." I hit him in the chest; he went back a few feet. His response was to charge me, and he caught me in the waist. In turn I grabbed him and flipped him in the air. At that instant, a teacher looked out his classroom door and saw him up in the air. The teacher opened the door and said, "What is going on here?"

Looking at the jock I replied, "He slipped, right?"

The jock shook his head yes, and the teacher said, "OK then, next time be careful," and shut the door.

I looked down and said, "Anytime, anywhere if you want to finish this." I turned and walked back to my sister, who was still standing there. I said, "Joanne, why aren't you in class?"

She replied, "I wanted to make sure you're OK." I laughed and told her not to worry about me as I walked her to class. Her teacher said, "You're late, Joanne."

I said that she wasn't feeling well and that I had to show her where the girls' room was. He replied, "OK, you get to your class."

CHAPTER 4

After that, things went back to normal for me, and by that, I mean no fighting. I did get to meet the small well-built Burnett. Her name was Eleanor, and she lived in O-Zone Park, which was 99 percent Italian. Things were going well. We would talk and flirt with each other between classes, but I could never walk her home or meet in the morning because of my detentions. One day, as we were going to lunch, she asked me to come over to her house sometime. I replied, "I'll come over tonight." She smiled, gave me her address, and told me to be over at about 6.

Her house was set behind a long driveway. The front had steps going to the front door, but they were not used. Instead it appeared that the side door was always used, partially because there were no lights in the front of the house. Eleanor was waiting for me by the front door, standing on the steps and making us the same height. She grabbed me and kissed me, saying, "I been waiting for a long time to do that." We both smiled, then we started making out. My hands slowly started moving over her body, and she didn't stop me. We were both becoming very excited, and my hand felt the moisture between her legs. She whispered in my ear, "Sit down and take it out, and I will sit on top of you."

I sat down and took it out, then she spread her legs and sat down on me. We rocked back-and-forth both lost in our excitement, climaxing together. We sat there not moving, just hugging and kissing. While kissing, she pulled back and said, "Pete you must promise me that I'll be the girl for you, no other girl." With my manhood rising I was quick to agree. She smiled, and we made love one more time.

Her mother opened the side door and said, "It's 9. Time to come in." We fixed ourselves, and she gave me a long kiss before heading for the side door. I walked down the driveway, smiling and thinking of having more sex.

I was brought back to reality when I saw six guys at the end of her driveway. The biggest one said, "Your name Wolfinger?"

I replied, "Since the day I was born."

He smiled and said, "My friend Tony here said you stole his girlfriend, and he wants revenge. So, you have two choices. One, you could join our gang the Saints. Win or lose, we will allow you in, so you can still see your Bella, in this all Italian neighborhood, even though you are not Italian. You can fight any member one on one. Or two, don't join, and fight all six of us at once, and don't come back to this neighborhood." I looked around, and I didn't like the odds, knowing the Quantrills were not hanging out together as much, and I didn't have much of a choice. I said I would join. He said, "Good, I heard of you. My name is Anthony. I'm president of the Ozone Park Chapter. We hang out at Rocky's Pizza on 101st Avenue, next to the Gambino Social Club. Be there this Friday. Now Tony, here is your chance for revenge."

They circled us. There was no noise, just me and Tony silently looking and sizing each other up. He looked small, chunky, and sneaky. He started cursing me; I just stood there looking at him smiling. He got mad and charged me. I saw he had knife in his right hand, and I was able to grab his hand with my left while kneeing him in the stomach. Then I started punching him in the head. He fell to the ground, dropping the knife. I quickly looked at my side and noticed my shirt was bloody. Before he could get up, I kicked him in the head and chest and stepped on his hand; he cried in pain and said, "I give up."

Anthony just smiled, turned to a guy named George, and said, "Didn't you say he said something to your girl? Do you want to fight him?" George looked at Tony then me and said, "No, I have no problem with him. If he wants her, he can have her."

Anthony said, "Good. See you Friday Wolfie." (That is how I got my nickname.)

As I was walking back home, I checked my side. It wasn't bad, just a flesh wound. I was more upset that he put a hole in my shirt.

The next day at school, I saw Eleanor. We kissed, and I asked her about Tony. She told me she had gone out with him, but she broke it off with him months ago. However, he would not let it go. "Are you jealous?" she asked, and, before I could answer, Lynn walked by, waved, and said, "Hi Pete." As I waved back, Eleanor pulled my hand down, reminding me to remember my promise. I smiled and said, "Who is jealous now? I'll see you at 6."

Eleanor replied, "You can't. I work at New Mark and Louis department store part time, and my father picks me up. I work Wednesdays and Fridays from 4-8 and Saturdays from 12-9. Come to Sunday dinner at about 5 and meet my family."

"OK," I replied.

On my way to her house that Sunday, I was passing a fruit store that was selling flowers. Wanting to make a good impression, I bought two bouquets. I arrived a little early, but I rang the bell anyway. Eleanor answered and told me to come inside. As I walked in, I gave her the flowers and said, "These are for you and your mother." Her mother was standing next to her and smiled.

Eleanor introduced me to everyone and told me to sit down and watch the soccer game with my father and brother while she and her sisters set the table. Her father said, "You watch soccer?"

I replied, "Not really."

Her father explained that today I was going to. It was a very important game; Italy was playing against Germany for the cup. After a few minutes, we were called to the table. Eleanor directed me to sit by her. The girls started serving us a salad, and everyone waited until everyone sat down, then we started to eat. The salad was followed by soup, then macaroni, and then the main dish, eggplant. I was stuffed after the macaroni, but I didn't want to be rude.

When dinner was finished, the father and son went back into the living room. Eleanor asked if she could be excused from helping do the dishes, and her mother obliged. Her sisters would do them.

Eleanor grabbed my hand while telling her mother that we would be sitting outside on the front steps. I sat down as she spread her dress and sat on top of my lap. After we finished having sex, we talked about what we were going to do after we graduated from school. We decided that we would get married; she would be a beautician, and I would be a plumber. Before we knew it, her mother leaned out the side door and said, "It is 9. Time to come in." We kissed and said goodnight. "See you in school tomorrow."

CHAPTER 5

It was a clear Friday night, great for walking to Rocky's Pizza. I arrived there at about 6, and there were about ten boys and girls hanging out in front of the store. They stopped and looked at me when Anthony came out and said, "Relax, this is Wolfie, and he is one of us." He continued, "Come in the store. I want to speak to you." Once we sat at the table, he said "Rocky only lets a few of us in at a time. I heard your father grew up with Patty, the bookie."

I replied, "Yes, and my great-grandmother was Catherine Zito."

Anthony replied, "Great. I have a great cousin name Zito; maybe we are related. Either way. I need you as one our leaders. You will be the fifth leader that will help run our organization. Because your rep as a fighter succeeds all the others, you will be my second, Sal third, Vito fourth, and Ralph fifth. Hate to use the word 'gang.' Here is a list of 65 members that go to Richmond Hill High school and their phone numbers. They were told that you are their leader. If you need them, call them. If you get a chance, meet them. Most likely half will run the other way if called upon. The main thing is I want you here with me. We have a lot of trouble with rivals. We run numbers and deliver money for the Gambino family. You have any trouble with that?"

I replied, "Nope. I'm good with that."

"We will then take the blood oath." Each of us cut our finger and mixed our blood, saying we would all be brothers forever. Once that was completed, Anthony continued, "Great. Get to know everyone. I have to meet someone." And he left.

I started to walk home, and I was about two blocks from Rocky's, in front of the bar where we ran numbers. I saw three of our members beating what looked like a gay man, so I stopped and I asked what they were doing. Steve replied, "Beating the gay motherfucker."

I said, "Stop."

Steve started to say fuck you, but before he could finish the sentence, I punched him in the stomach, then backhanded him on the side of the head. He fell to his knees. The gay man was crying. "They … they took all my money and the cross my mother gave me."

I turned and said, "Who took the cross?" A member named Tom held it out in his hand, and I commanded, "Give it back. Then go into the bar and tell the bartender to send a cab."

The cab came in what seemed like seconds. We threw the gay man in the cab and told the cab driver to take off. I then turned to the three members and said, "You are all assholes. Did you ever think what could come of this if he talks to someone? All of you better hope he doesn't."

I started to walk home again, and before I knew it, I was opening the door to my apartment. While walking into the bedroom, I saw my mother and her sister, Aunt Grace, drinking. They were both drunk; my Aunt Grace said, "Come here and give me a kiss." I passed without stopping and went into the bedroom. My brothers were already sleeping. I undressed and fell into bed, hearing my Aunt Grace telling my mother if she didn't start disciplining me, she would find me in an alley dead before I turned 21. Before I could hear my mother's response, I fell asleep.

It was a Friday night, and Anthony was paying everyone for their services. A member came in and said, "We have a problem. You are needed down in the 102nd Street Park."

Anthony turned to me and told me to handle it. "I'll be there as soon as I can." The park was about three blocks south of Rocky's Pizza; it took only a few minutes to get there. I arrived to see a Black kid on the ground and three of our members climbing on the Cyclone fence then jumping on him. I ordered them to stop and demanded they tell me what happened. Tom came forward and said, "This spook tried to grab the money bag from Sal, but a few of us caught him. He is a member of the Mau Mau Chaplains out of Brooklyn." They stood him up, and I walked over to him, but I knew he wasn't going to talk. It looked like his jaw was broken, so I ordered them to bring him over to the train station and drop him there before they went home.

I went back to Rocky's. Anthony was still there, the song "La Bamba" was playing in the jukebox as I brought him up to date. Anthony asked for suggestions on how to handle the situation. I replied, "Let's start by never taking the same route twice, and when carrying cash, we should have one member hang back until delivery."

Anthony agreed, "Good idea. Let's do that, and I'll talk to the boss. OK, let's call it a night. Everyone watch their backs."

The next day Anthony instructed a member called Nut to watch the door while he informed us what he had learned. The Genovese family was trying to take over the Gambino numbers territory and was using the Brooklyn gangs to invade our territory. The five of us had begun discussing what to do next when a firebomb crashed through the window. Within seconds, we ran out the front door as the flames spread across the store's floor. We saw a Caddy take off, and before I knew it Nut raised a shotgun, shooting the back of the Caddy. The Caddy hit a pole, but no one got out. My ears were ringing from the shotgun blast. Looking around, I could hear the sirens coming and see the flames coming out of the store. And Nut was just standing there. Anthony said, "Let's split. Meet at the park tomorrow around 7." Everyone started to run, except Nut; he was just standing there, so I pulled on his shirt while saying, "Let's go." As we were running, we realized he still had the shotgun, and I told him to throw it down the sewer. We had to keep moving. When we got to 109th Avenue, we went our separate ways.

I woke up with my mother telling me that Eleanor had called and would like to see me at 11. I thanked her for passing on the message, then I got dressed and headed to the door. I arrived at her house at about 11 and saw her waiting on the front steps. When she saw me, her face lit up, and she ran to me, and when she got to me, she started to hug and kiss me. We walked back to the front steps, and I sat down, then she spread out her dress and sat down on my lap while telling me she was worried because the news said two Black gang members were seriously injured in a car accident and Rocky's Pizza was set on fire. They believed both incidents were gang related. I replied, "And what does that have to do with me?"

Eleanor said, "My brother told me you are a captain in the Saint gang and second in command, and Tony stabbed you in a fight over me. Please, tell me if it is true. I see how the guys look at you in school; sometimes I think they're going to kiss your ring."

I laughed and said, "You should be more worried about the girls that look at me."

"I am," she replied.

I said, "Yes, I'm a member. That was only the way I could see you without having my head handed to me. And yes, Tony did stab me, but believe me, he got the worst of it, and I'm not that important. Remember, I'm Irish and German and Italian, and the leaders are 100 percent Italian." I started to kiss her while I slipped my hand under her dress, feeling her moist womanhood. I then took my manhood and pleased her with it. When we both were completely satisfied, we rested in each other's arms, caught in our own dreams. Then her mother said, "Time for dinner."

As we got up, she grabbed me and said, "Remember I love you and always will.

I gently took her in my arms while kissing her and said, "I'm yours forever, see you tomorrow in school."

After leaving her, I went directly to the park; the council was waiting for me. As I entered the circle, Anthony started talking. He had been informed that all the Brooklyn gangs would gather together and attack us tomorrow night around 8. "They will be coming in cars and on the train. Get the word out to everyone to meet at Rockaway and Liberty Ave. around 7. Even if they don't show, we have to be ready. Also, the elders were very happy with the hijacking from Kenny airport diner; expect a reward. OK, see everyone tomorrow."

CHAPTER 6

I woke up, got dressed, had some breakfast, and started for school, wondering what was going to happen when we met Brooklyn tonight. I waited for Eleanor before class, but she never showed up. I thought to myself, "She might have woken up late. I'll catch her at lunch.

Lunchtime came, and she wasn't there. I went to a pay phone and called her house. Her mother answered. I said, "Hello, is Eleanor there?"

"She is not and will be home very late."

I said, "OK, please tell her I'll see here tomorrow then."

Her mother replied, "I will give her the message," and hung up. The day went by fast. I reached out to my members and told them where to be at 7. Most of them said they would be there. After school I went home, grabbed a bite, and started for the meeting spot; I walked by Eleanor's house and noticed a strange car in the driveway. "It's probably a friend of her brother," I said to myself as I walked by.

I met with the counselors at Rockaway Avenue at about 6:45, and we already had about 50 members there. Anthony said, "I bet they don't show." By now there were cop cars all over. At about 9 p.m., Anthony gave the order to go home. The five of us started walking back to Rocky's Pizza. When we got to 103rd Avenue, I said to Anthony, "I'm heading home," and started to head home. Just then about four unmarked police pulled up to the group, got out, and said, "Hands up." Since I was about 10 feet away, I kept walking. I heard, "Halt, or I'll shoot." I truly didn't believe he was talking to me, so I kept walking. Then Anthony hollered out, "Wolfie, stop. He will shoot."

I stopped and turned around and saw a gun pointed at me. The cop said, "Your buddy just saved your life. Another second and I would have shot you. One less punk in this world. Now get over here."

As we were being handcuffed, Sal asked, "What are we being arrested for?"

The cop replied, "Murder." They put us in their patrol cars and brought us to the 102nd Precinct, where they fingerprinted us then put us in the holding pen.

Once we were all there, Anthony said, "Remember, say nothing. Only talk to your lawyer."

The next morning an officer came, woke us, and let us go. "You're going to Brooklyn for arraignment, and 1010 WINS radio, the press, parents, and everyone else is out there, waiting to see you. My advice is keep your mouth shut and get in the van." As we were getting into the van, I spotted my mother and father. My mother was crying; my father looked like if he could get his hands on me, he would beat the shit out of me.

Once in court, we all sat in the first row; our lawyers were there. I recognized Jake Newell, my father's lawyer. All the lawyers were standing in front of judge. I heard the judge say, "Bail denied," then he banged the gavel, got up, and walked out. The jailer said, "OK let's go." We all walked into the holding pen. Ralph asked where we were going. The jailer replied, "To the Brooklyn House of Detention, known as 'The Tombs.'"

Sal said, "I have a cousin that's there. He's an orderly."

We all piled into the van and headed for the tombs. On the way, they picked up about five more guys. We arrived about hour later. We were taken out of the van and marched single file into a large room. We were told be quiet while the officers filled out the paperwork. While standing there, the guy behind me grabbed my ass. I quickly turned and hit him on the side of his head. The blow sent him out of the line. Hearing the noise, the guard turned and said, "Stay in line." The guy, now with a frightened face, stepped back in line, apologizing and saying that when he saw the pants and my good looks, he thought I was gay.

I turned and said, "These pants are called chinos, and my looks I was born with."

Sal started laughing. "Well we always knew the girls love you, but now the guys do too."

I replied, "Fuck you."

Sal replied, "See you already turning." We all started laughing; the guard turned and said, "I said no talking."

We marched into a large room. Once we were all in, the guard said, "Strip down to your birthday suit, and lay your clothes in front of you, then turn around, bend over, and spread those cheeks. I will be looking up your ass with a flashlight. Any farts when I'm inspecting you, and I will stick this flashlight up your ass. Now, let's get started." When he finished, he told us to turn around. "When the doc comes in, hold out your arms for inspection. He will ask questions. Answer 'yes' or 'no.'"

The doctor came in and started inspecting us one by one. He stopped in front of a guy that was obviously on drugs. The doc asked, "Are you on drugs?"

He replied, "No." The Doc didn't say a thing; he moved to the next guy. Finally, he got to me. While inspecting me, he said, "I see the Lord blessed you with everything but a brain." Then he moved on to the next guy. When the doctor was finished, the guard said, "Get dressed." We then marched until we came to a window, where we stopped.

The guard said, "You will receive one blanket, one pillow, one roll of toilet paper, one bar of soap, and will be assigned to a cell. You will be allowed to shower once a week. When you hear a click, your cell gate will unlock, and you will have 10 seconds to leave your cell and stand in front of your cell before it locks. You are not allowed to receive any packages; you may have money put into an account, and that money can be used in our Commissary. Now let's get moving."

CHAPTER 7

There were about 20 cells to a cellblock. When the guard saw an empty cell or bed, he would stop and unlock the cell, and one of us would enter. He would then write down the name and lock the cell, and we would move on. I was the last one, and I would be sharing a cell. While opening the cell the guard said, "Albert, I have a play mate for you, so play nice." He locked the gate and walked away. I looked around and saw bunk beds, a sink, and a toilet. Albert said, "The bottom bed is mine."

I replied, "No problem," and started walking toward the beds. Then Sal hollered out that we had made the papers and he was sending one down so I could read it. Sal was two cells from me. I turned around and started for the front of the cell. Albert got the paper first, looked at it, and loudly said, "You're a leader of the Saints?"

I replied, "Not really. Anthony is the leader. I'm just a captain."

He screamed, "I'm going to kill you," as he charged me. The cellblock stared chanting "Fight, fight." Before I could raise my hands, he had me in a bear hug. I spit in his face, but he didn't loosen his grip. I pulled my head back, then with all I could muster I hit his nose with my forehead. We heard a pop, and the blood came out. He relaxed his grip, letting me free. I started to punching him. He started returning punches. When he was close enough, he stopped punching and grabbed me in a headlock. He started to squeeze my neck; I couldn't break his hands free, so I grabbed his nuts and started squeezing them. He let go, screaming. He was slightly bent over, holding his nuts. I put my two fists together and came up, hitting the bottom of his chin and jerking his head back. This caused him to fall backward on the floor. I then jumped on his chest with my knees, and at the same time, I lifted my left hand and came down with a fist, hitting his cheek. I was about to do it again when I felt a nightstick on my throat pulling me off. I heard a guard telling me to get up and stand in the corner. The guard then looked at Albert and asked the other guard to check him. The other guard kicked him hard in the ribs; Albert moaned. The guard said, "He's alive." Then they both looked at me. (I said to myself, "I'm fucked.") One guard said, "Get your stuff. We're moving you." I got my stuff and started walking past Albert; he still was still laying on the ground, moaning. The guard opened the gate. They marched me down the cellblock. I passed by friends, but no one said a word. They opened the gate and ordered me to get in. "Remember, you fell" Then they locked the gate and left. I fell on the bed and went to sleep.

I woke up feeling cold. I looked around; it was dark and quiet. I put my blanket over me and went back to sleep. I woke up to the sound of someone screaming out that he was sick. I got up and went to the sink to wash up. I looked into a small mirror that was nailed to the wall. What I saw was not good. I had a black eye and cuts and bruises on my face, hands, and arms. I looked a mess. I was standing there when I heard the gate click open. I ran to the gate, opened it, and stepped out. The guards marched us to the mess hall. It was like school; you took a tray and followed the guy in front of you, taking from what was displayed. I grabbed a box of cereal, a container of milk, juice, and an apple. I also grabbed a plastic spoon, then sat down with my friends.

Anthony said, "You look like you had a tough day."

Sal said, "They carried Albert out on a stretcher."

Vito said, "Did you see we made the paper?"

Ralph said, "Fuck it all." We looked at each other and laughed. We did idle talk because no one had heard anything new. The horn sounded; we stood up, marched back to our cells, and on the way out we disposed of our garage and trays. Once in my cell, I lay down, falling asleep looking up at the ceiling. I woke up to a click of the gate. I opened the gate and stood outside. We were marched to a day room and released in that room. While I was looking around, I said to myself, "I must have missed lunch." I saw a group of guys playing cards, and there were a few benches in front of a TV with *American Bandstand* playing on it. A group of guys were yelling which girl they would fuck. The loud speaker came on saying, "If anyone takes their dick out, I will beat it off with my nightstick." I walked to my friends, and we stood there looking around. Sal pointed to a guy sitting on the floor, looking like he'd pissed and shit himself. All his veins were showing and looked purple. I said, "Looks like the dope addict that came in with us." Then two guards came in and dragged him out. The horn sounded, the gate opened, and we marched back to our cells. At about 5 o'clock, the gate clicked open, and we marched to dinner, then back to our cells. This was the daily routine. Saturday came, and I took my shower. If you spent less than ten minutes in the showers, the guys would start hollering that you were still dirty.

Sunday came, and my mother came to visit. She picked up the phone, crying and saying I looked pale. She had brought me some things, but they wouldn't take them. I explained that she had to put money in account, so I could buy things I needed. She said the officer told her that. I asked where Dad was, and she told me that he was outside waiting in the car. She said the police found the killer, and they may drop the charges to disorderly and unlawful assembly, but the bail was still high. Then she started crying. I said, "Don't worry mom. I'm OK."

The guard said, "Time is up." I blew her a kiss as I walked away. The days turned into daily routines, then weeks. Once in a while, someone would act up. One time, while we were having dinner, a 6'6", 400-hundred-pound weight lifter didn't like the food, so he picked up the table and threw it, then started hitting the other prisoners. The guards ran outside the room and locked the door. I did not blame him; the chicken looked gray. I gave mine to someone for two cigarettes. After he calmed down, the door opened and about four guards as big as him came in and started beating him, then cuffed him. Once that was done, everything went back to normal.

It was night the beginning of the third week; I was lying in bed, listening to someone singing when someone said, "Stop singing."

The singer said, "Who said that?"

"Upper C10," came the reply.

The singer said, "This lower C12. I'll see you in the day room."

The next day we marched to the day room. I went to the corner where my friends were and told them what happened. We waited and watched. Two guys came into the center of the room, holding a pencil in each hand and talking in Spanish. They circled each other, trying to poke out the other guy's eye. Then one hit the card table, knocking it over. That's when holy hell broke loose. We stood in the corner watching; the guards came in swinging. Once they got everything under control, they marched us back to our cells.

It was early Saturday morning. The guard unlocked my cell and told me to go with him. We went to a holding room, and my friends were there also. Anthony said, "All the charges were dropped. Our parents had to sign that they would not sue for false arrest. We are being released!" Everyone was yelling, "Thank God."

I said, "Anthony, I need to speak to you." We moved over to a corner. I continued. "Anthony, I'm not coming back."

He said, "No one quits."

I said, "Anthony, if you want to have it out, we will, but please listen to my side first." He nodded his head. I said, "We both know you will rise, and so will your other captains. I cannot because I'm not 100 percent Italian. I know you will always have my back, but you and I both know the day will come when you will have to choose, and we know it won't be me. You saved my life. I promise you, as a brother, no matter how long or where, I will be there for you when you ask me to save your life." I held out my hand; he looked at me, then grabbed and hugged me while whispering, "You will be missed."

A guard called his name and told him where to sign on a piece of paper. When he was done, he was told that his parents were waiting for him. As each one left, we said our goodbyes. I was the last one. The guard said, "Sign here. Your father is waiting."

I said, "No thanks."

The guard replied, "If you don't sign, I cannot release you."

I replied, "I would rather stay here than have my father beat me."

He said, "OK," and walked away. He came back laughing, saying, "Your mother promised he won't kill you."

I signed the papers. Once outside, it felt great to breathe in fresh air. My mother couldn't stop hugging and kissing me; my father looked at me and said, "Help your mother into the car." I turned to help her when I felt a blow on the back of my head, bringing me down to my knees. My mother jumped out of the car, hitting my father and saying, "You promised."

My father picked me up by my collar, saying, "Tell your mother you tripped," as he threw me in the back seat. I told my mom I had tripped. When we got home, everyone but Eleanor was in the apartment waiting for me. They were telling me how much they missed me. I thanked everyone, and after a while, everyone went their own way. I sat down and had something to eat. My grandmother and mother watched and kept asking me if I wanted more. I said, "No thank you." I finished, got up, hugged them both, then went next door. My grandfather was sitting at the kitchen table, cleaning a fish. I walked over and hugged him, saying, "Thank you for teaching me how to fight. I love you."

He looked up and said, "I love you too," I left grandpa and went down to the shop.

As I walked in, my father was sitting at his desk doing paperwork; I walked over and sat down. He turned toward me, apologizing for hitting me. I replied that I was sorry for causing him so much trouble and told him I deserved him hitting me. He stood up; I said to myself, "Here comes another shot," but he put his arms around me and said, "I'm glad you're safe. Now go up and get some rest."

CHAPTER 8

I woke the next morning feeling great. It was Sunday morning, which meant Eleanor was home. I called and told her I would be over at about 10. She said, "I'll be waiting on the front step."

When she saw me, she ran to me, crying and saying she missed me. I hugged her and told her everything was OK now. She looked at me and said, "I'm pregnant."

I looked down at her and said, "No problem. I'll quit school, and we will get married. I'll go to work with my father."

She replied saying, "It will never work. I'll always love you, but I'm getting married to someone else next week." Crying hysterically, she turned and ran into her house. Her father and brother came out and said, "Please leave and don't bother Eleanor anymore."

I stood there in shock, not sure what had just happened. I turned and started to walk home; I stopped at a few pay phones and tried calling her, but no one would answer. My heart felt like it was breaking. When I got home, my father called me into the shop and asked me to sit down. I was crying as I sat down; he said, "Eleanor called and asked you to stop calling her." Before I could say anything, he said, "You cannot keep a woman if she does not want to be kept. You could put her in a closet, lock it, put two guards in front, and when you open it, you will find her with the man she wants."

I said, "Dad, my heart feels like it is breaking; it hurts so much."

My father replied, "Nothing you can do but go on with life. Your heart will heal, I promise, and you will meet someone that will love you as much as you love her. Now go upstairs and get ready for school tomorrow; it is a big day. We have to make sure we get you back in school."

I entered my bedroom, turned on my record player, and started playing "A Teenager in Love." I softly sang the words while I undressed, and lay in my bed crying softly. I was thinking of what I did wrong. My heart ached, but finally I was getting sleepy. I said to myself, "Once I sleep, the pain will stop."

I woke up feeling sad, and my heart ached whenever I would think of Eleanor. I looked around my room and saw that my mother had polished my shoes, pressed my shirt and pants, and set out a green tie hanging on my shirt. "My grandmother came from Ireland, and my mother believed that the color green was lucky," she said as I got out of bed. I got dressed, and I walked out the door, hugging and kissing my mother as I passed her. My grandma was waiting at her door also, so I hugged and kissed her too, saying, "Thank you. Love you both."

My father and I walked into the principal's main office and saw Mrs. Koch sitting in her private office. My father told me to sit as he walked into her private office and shut the door. The secretary and I could hear that a heated conversation was taking place, when all of sudden, my father slammed his hand down on the desk and said "I'm a taxpayer. My son was found innocent of all charges. Maybe you would want tell the press why you are discriminating against him." Mrs. Koch said something to him, which I couldn't hear, then my father opened the door and said to me, "Get to class. If you get in any more trouble, I'll make sure where you came from looks like a picnic." He then shut the door and continued to talk to Mrs. Koch.

I picked up my books and went to my first class. I entered the room and sat in my assigned seat. The teacher said nothing. I looked over where Eleanor sat, and my heart ached. When the class ended, I asked the teacher if there was any way I could make up the work I had missed. He smiled and said he would have something for me the next day. I asked every teacher the same thing and received the same answer.

I went to lunch, and my friends were still there. When they saw me, they all smiled. LeRoy said, "I bet you had your hands full."

Paul said, "What does he mean?"

Jack said, "It means he ran a lot." We looked at Paul's puzzled face, and everyone laughed.

The third day I ran into Anna, Eleanor's best friend. She said, "Eleanor is getting married today, and she told me the baby's is yours."

I said, "Anna, I asked for her to marry me. She said no. What more could I do? I didn't even know she was seeing someone else."

Anna inquired, "She didn't tell you anything?"

"Nope."

Anna started to walk away, but as she walked, she turned and said, "Eleanor loves you more than you will ever know." Then she kept walking. I stood there, not understanding what she meant. I did see Anna every so often, and when I did, she would turn her head the other way. I thought to myself, "Now that is a friend."

I started playing cards after school with my fellow classmates and friends for some money. Once in a while, I would work a Saturday with my father. There were plenty of girls who wanted to date me; I tried, but it wasn't the same. I would go on one date but never a second time with the same girl. On occasion, I would hang out at the Imperial Bar with my old Quantrills friends and at Grace's Candy Store, where the decent girls hung out, including my sister.

CHAPTER 9

After a few years, I graduated, which surprised a lot of people. Jim the bartender signed my yearbook, writing "Best of beers." I got my license and started saving for car. I would hang out in the Imperial on Friday and Saturday nights, then Grace's during the days and on Sundays.

One night, Joe, the owner of the bar, said he was going to start a dance hall in the back and asked if I would keep it from getting out of hand for a small fee. I accepted his offer. He replied, "Great! It will start next week. Your buddy, Big Tony, will be playing with his band."

During the week I would split my time between the two hangouts. One night I was outside the bar having a smoke when I heard someone ask, "Why are you always sad?" I turned to see a young girl, maybe 14 or 15 years old, and her mother sitting in front of the building next to the bar. I walked over and said, "Hello. I'm not sad."

I noticed that she had a pretty young face as she replied, "Well you looked sad. I see you when you take those pretty girls out; you show no feelings."

I smiled as I replied, "So you been watching me?"

She replied, "Yes. I'm 15, and I have graduated with a PhD in Psychology. I find you very interesting You're tall, handsome, and you look kind and smart."

I said, "Well then I cannot think of a better reason."

She responded, "My name is Cookie because I'm so smart. I get very bad headaches, and no one knows why."

I replied, "I'm sorry to hear that."

"Thank you. The doctors are working on it. I like to sit out here to view people and listen to music. It helps me. I spoke to you because you come out with the most different women, and I would like to talk to you more," continued Cookie.

I replied, "Don't let Charlie hear. He thinks he's the ladies' man." As I concluded our conversation Jim came out of the bar and told me that I was needed inside. I told him I would head that way, then I turned to Cookie and said, "Hold that thought."

I came into the bar saying, "What's the problem?" Jim directed me to the backroom. I went to the back a saw a crowd of girls screaming, "Stop." I broke through to see a big guy over a girl, hitting her. I grabbed his hair, pulling his head back and chopping his throat. He turned and saw me holding his throat. I then hit him with three fast punches to the stomach. He bent over, and I put both my hands together, swinging them up and hitting him under the chin. His head hit the back wall, and he started to slide down to the floor. I kept hitting him until he was on the floor. I told Tony to open the side door, and I dragged the guy outside and laid him on the sidewalk. I then kicked him a few times in the stomach. I walked back in, locking the side door. As I went back into the room, I asked the girls to help the girl into the ladies' room and to clean her up.

Jim asked if everything was OK, and I gave the thumbs up. We sat there having idle talk, when a girl came up to me and told me that Lori, the girl who had been attacked, wanted to talk to me, so I told Jim I would talk to him later and I headed to the girl in the backroom. Lori ran up to me telling me that she had no ride home and was scared of what her parents would say and do to her. I said, "OK, come with me." We walked into the bar room, and I asked Jim to borrow his badge and car. Jim was a retired cop, and I had come up with a plan to help Lori. While Jim was giving me the badge and keys, he reminded me not to lose the badge, but he never asked me why I wanted it in the first place. Lori and I went out the front, and then I helped her in the car. I looked over to see Cookie, staring at me and writing in her book. I waved before getting into the car. Lori told me where she lived, and as we were driving, I told her the plan. She agreed to my plan and hugged me. I said, "Hope it works."

I rang the front door bell, and I heard the father asking someone in the house who would ring the bell at this time of night followed by, "Marta get the door." Her mother answered the door. Seeing her daughter, she put her hand to her mouth and said, "Oh dear. What happened?"

Hearing that, Lori's father came to the door. I flashed the badge and said, "Detective Peter Tulles. Sorry sir, but your daughter was a target of a mugging. The mugger got away, but your daughter put up a brave fight."

Lori said, "Please, let the police officer go. I want to go to bed."

"OK, thank you officer." Then her parents shut the door.

I got into the car and said, "You're now on you own, Lori." I went back to the bar to give Jim his badge and keys back. Jim said, "Someone called the ambulance for the guy outside. Joe said stay away from his niece next door, or you'll look like the guy you just beat up." I told him that I would see him tomorrow. I started walking home, and for whatever reason I started to think of Eleanor. My heart started to hurt, so I tried putting her out of my mind the only way I knew how: I fell in my bed and went to sleep.

CHAPTER 10

It was a beautiful Saturday morning as I walked to Grace's Candy Store. When I got there, I went to the jukebox, put my quarter in, and pressed 12 for "Sealed with a Kiss." As I sat down and ordered a large egg cream, I was still thinking about what I did wrong with Eleanor. Eventually, my heart hurt, so I tried thinking of something else. I looked around the room, and all the faces were the same, except for one. Her name was Donna, and she had come with her brother, George. Seeing me, she walked up to me and said, "My brother says you're a nice guy. I have a party to go to. Will you take me?" I responded by telling her that I had no car, usually, and when I did, it was a beat up 1952 Cadillac, Donna replied, "Great, here's my address."

As she left with her brother, Lester said, "You lucky dog. I was going to ask her out."

"Maybe next time," I teased. I left and started walking back home. I was thinking that Donna looked like Eleanor, and my heart started to hurt. Before I knew it, I found myself in front of the Imperial. I went in, sat down, and started talking with a few of the boys. While we were hanging out, a football team came in with their girlfriends; they were celebrating a victory. The football guys didn't want to dance, so the girls said that they would ask my friends and me. Their reply was, "Who cares?"

With that the football captain's girlfriend came up to me and said, "My names Pat. Want to dance?" I signaled that I didn't want to; the girls didn't get mad. Instead, they started dancing with each other. I went outside for a smoke and saw Cookie sitting there, looking sad. I walked over and said, "Now who looks sad?"

She looked up and smiled, saying, "We are moving to Maryland. There is a university there that may be able to help me while I study."

I said, "That is great!" Hearing the music from the bar, I continued, "Let's celebrate. Come on, let's dance."

Cookie asked, "Here?"

I said, "Why not?" I grabbed her hand, pulling her from her chair.

She sheepishly admitted, "I don't know how to dance."

"It's easy. Here, let me show you," I offered as a slow song came on. To the song "Love Me Tender," I put her arms around me and pulled her close. She looked up, smiled, and put her head on my chest. She went into her own world as we swayed to the music. Finally, she looked up and said, "This is my first dance, and I have never been kissed."

I said, "I don't believe that, but I'll fix that." I gently raised her chin with my finger. I bent down to kiss her; our lips met, and her lips were warm, moist, and tender. As I lifted my head, I noticed her eyes were closed and the music had stopped. I asked, "How was that?"

She softly replied, "Very nice. I have to go in now." She turned and went into the apartment. I thought I heard her crying and saying, "You will always be my first love." Little did I know that would be the last time that I would see her.

The football crowd came out and began getting in their cars. While Pat was getting into the car, she turned to me smiling and said, "I will have that dance."

Donna's house was huge mansion in Kew Gardens Estates. I walked up the steps, rang the bell, and waited. A maid answered and asked, "Who is calling?"

I replied, "Donna's date." I heard a deep voice instructing her to let me come in. I walked in and was led to the rear of house and into a large den. I saw a big man holding a cigar and a glass of wine, looking at a large television. He turned and said, "Sit." So, I sat. "What is your name?" I told him; then Donna walked in and said, "Let's go."

I got up and said, "Pleased meeting you sir."

He said, "Be good."

Donna held her hand out, and her father put twenty dollars in it before turning back the television. As we got into the car, she gave me the 20, but I gave it back and told her to never do that again. She argued, "Why not use it for gas?"

"I said no! Now where is the party?"

Donna replied, "There isn't any. I said that to get you to take me out. Let's go to the drive-in."

After that we dated for about three weeks, and I only got to third base with her.

One night I was picking up Donna when the maid said, "Mr. D'Agostino said he would like to see you, sir." I walked into the study, and her father told me to sit down. "How about a drink?" I politely declined, so he continued. "How would you like to be in the plumber's union?"

I said, "Thank you, sir. I would have to think about it because I work with my father."

He replied, "No problem."

Donna and I got into the car, heading to Grace's Ice Cream Shop. I told her what her father said and asked if she knew why he was being so generous. Donna replied, "Sure. I told him we were engaged."

"What are you nuts?" I exclaimed. "I never asked you. I'm only 18."

Donna replied, "I let you touch me."

I said, "That is called petting. I didn't fuck you or get you pregnant."

Donna said, "I don't care. I want you." I turned the car around and pulled back in front of her house. I told her that you cannot buy love, so she got out of the car and ran into the house crying.

The next night after work I stopped at the Imperial. Jim said, "Where have you been? Two tough looking guys with Italian accents were looking for you, and the football girls have been coming in here. The tall red head was asking for you."

I replied, "I've been busy."

Jim smiled and said, "I bet you were."

I left and went to Grace's, and Grace said, "You just missed two tough looking guys with Italian accents; they we're looking for you. What did you do?" I told her that I had done nothing. I decided to go home.

I saw my father in the shop and told him what happened. He said, "I want you to walk around the block and think about this. She is pretty and wealthy, and her father is a very powerful person. You would have every-thing a person would want. Now go and walk around the block."

After walking around the block, I said, "Dad, I know what you're saying, but I don't love her. I want to marry for love not money."

He said, "OK. If they come around here, we will have kill a wop hour. Better go to bed; we have a boiler to put in tomorrow."

The next day after work, I was in the Imperial when Lester came in. He saw me and said, "I heard you and Donna broke up. Is it OK if I ask her out?"

I said, "Please be my guest, the quicker the better."

He said, "I'll call her right now."

I gave him her number and a dime; he took them, went into the phone booth, and came out smiling. "See you later," he said as he walked out.

Jim the bartender said, "You are one lucky bastard."

I said, "You better believe it."

CHAPTER 11

I was sitting in the Imperial Bar, nursing a drink and wondering where to get some money for my Saturday night date with a model named Janet. We had met in Gertz Department Store when I was looking for a shirt and she was modeling a new clothing line. I walked by while she was modeling on the walking way. She looked at me, and I waved to her. She waved back to me when she went back behind the curtain. I had started to walk away, but a girl came out and asked if I would wait. I told her that I would, and eventually, Janet came out and introduced herself. I did the same, and she said that it was nice to look at a person the same height as her. I laughed and agreed with her. Then I asked, "How about going over to Teddy's for a cup of coffee?"

She said, "I would love to, but I have a to finish the show. Here is my number and address. Pick me up at 7 on Saturday." Then she turned and left.

As I was thinking back on our meeting, Fingers came in the bar looking for a partner for Street Roulette. He asked and said that it was an opportunity that paid well.

Figuring it was just racing, I said, "I'll try it."

John responded, "Great, meet me at 6 tonight at Atlantic Avenue and 111th Street."

I got there about ten minutes to 6 and saw a crowd at the corner. There was also a bookie in the middle of the crowd taking money. I walked over to John and asked, "What are we doing? And what car are we using?"

John said, "Mine. With my missing fingers, I cannot hold the steering wheel tight, so I will be your wingman. When I say right, you move to the left. You move to the left, giving the car coming from the right time to break. Should you hit the brakes or a car, we lose. We have to drive through Atlantic Avenue, 95th Avenue, 101st Avenue, 103rd Avenue, and Liberty Avenue. No beeping the horn, but I disconnected the horn in case you hit it. Just to let you know, the odds are against us, but if we win, we are in the money."

We walked over to John's car, a nice '55 Chevy fully worked out. I got in and adjusted the seat and radio. The song "Wipe Out" was playing, so I looked at John, and we both started laughing. I said, "Ready?"

John merely replied, "When the light changes red, we go."

I said to myself, "This is one-sided." I started power braking, creating a lot of smoke and making the cars passing slow down. The light changed red, so I released my foot from the brake and put the pedal to the metal. The car reared up, and we shot off like a bullet. Even though the cars on Atlantic Avenue had the right of way, they all were stopped looking at us, which gave us enough time to cross through the intersection. The next crossing was 95th Avenue, and we flew by no problem. We continued to 101st Avenue, and while I was crossing, John hollered, "Right!"

I swung into the left lane of oncoming traffic to avoid a car before coming back in my lane. As we came up to 109th Avenue, we flew right across the road; it was a four-way stop sign, so the cars saw us approaching and let us through. We were coming up to Liberty Ave., the most dangerous of them all. As we approached the street, the light was against us. I felt for sure we were going to get hit, but just as we got to the light, it changed in our favor. Green! When we were able to stop, I got out of the car, and my legs were shaking. John said to me, "So who is Eleanor?" When I asked why, he informed me that I had screamed, "Fuck you Eleanor," and nailed the gas.

I told him that she was just a girl that I knew once a long time ago. "Now, let's get our money." The bookie was not happy, but he paid us each $300 and said he was moving the race to a new location.

John asked, "Wolfie, you in?"

"No, being an asshole once is enough for me."

Saturday night came, and I picked up the model, Janet, for our date. She was wearing a nice dress and flats for shoes; her hair was up, and she asked me if it bothered me because it made her look taller. I told her it didn't; then, we went to the Imperial Bar for some dancing and drinking. Eventually, we left the bar, found a nice spot, and started making out.

I slid my hand up her dress and found her to be moist. I took my manhood out, and she grabbed it while whispering in my ear, "You pleasure me, and I pleasure you." I felt her climax, then she put her hand over the top of manhood when I was exploding, keeping it from going all over the car. She smiled and asked if I had a handkerchief, then started kissing me again. "I never give in totally on the first date," she admitted. We made out for a while before I drove her home early because she was flying out for a modeling job in California the next day. She said she would call me when she got back and asked for my number. I gave it to her with one number wrong, saying, "I'll be waiting." I got into the car, thinking it had been nice, but something was missing, just like with the rest of the girls I dated.

CHAPTER 12

A few days later, my friends and I were sitting in the bar when we heard Johnny Fingers was killed and Tom had been seriously injured playing street roulette. They were coming out of the 134th Street Tunnel, and the car slid under a milk truck.

The only ones at the funeral were the old gang and some friends. Looking at the coffin, I could almost hear Johnny saying, "You can't knock it if you haven't tried it."

After the funeral, I was sitting in the bar, waiting for the back-room dancing room to open. Suddenly, I heard, "There you are handsome." I turned and saw a tall, pretty redhead coming toward me with a few other girls behind her. She grabbed my face and kissed me; her lips tasted sweet. I pulled back and said, "Hi!"

She replied, "Hi yourself. I have been coming here and waiting for you. Where have you been? Chasing other pretty girls?"

I smiled and said, "I've been busy, and aren't you the football captain's girl?

She replied, "He said I'm not anymore."

"If you say so," I replied as I looked around, watching her girlfriends making friends. I continued, "My name is Wolfie."

She replied, "Mine is Pat." With the formals out of the way, we headed to the backroom. I introduced her to Big Tony, then we made our way to a table away from the band. We really had a nice time, and I asked if I could see her again. She said yes and gave me her telephone number. We went out a few more times, and I even took her to the Moose Club dance. Then one night after making passionate love, she said to me, "My boyfriend in Florida asked me to marry him and move to Florida."

"What did you say?"

"What do you want me to say?"

I replied, "What you heart tells you. While I understand you are a few years older than me but do not look it, I'm 18, so I'm not looking for marriage." She looked hurt and asked me to take her home. We kissed goodnight before she got out of the car and ran into her house crying.

The following Sunday afternoon, I was sitting at the bar, talking to some of my friends, and listening to the song "Peppermint Twist" when the front flew door open and the football team came in. They lined across the front of the wall, and the captain stepped forward. Looking at Big Tony, he asked, "Who is Wolfie?" Tony pointed to me, then the captain looked at Jim and he pointed to me. I smiled and said, "How can I help you? I don't play football."

The captain said, "My girl said you kept making passes at her and won't leave her alone."

"She is pretty," I responded.

The captain then charged me with the rest of the team following toward my friends. I picked up the bar stool, pushed the cushion seat in his stomach, and raised the chair, bringing it up and putting it over his head. The stool missed his head, but the bars of the stool hit his shoulder pads, making him buckle. He returned by springing up with an upper cut, catching me under the chin and sending me sliding across the table. I took the tablecloth with me as I hit the back wall.

When I woke up, everything was over. Looking around I saw Jim having his leg bandaged; he looked over at me laughing and asked, "Done with your nap?" I continued to look around, noticing Big Tony with his arm in a sling, Charlie with an ice bag over his eye, and Lester with an ice bag on his head. Al said it was like hitting uniforms with armored plates in them. I got up and helped clean the mess up. Once we finished, I started for home. I passed the shop before going upstairs and saw my father was inside. I entered the shop, walked back to his desk, and sat in a chair. I said, "Hi Dad, working late are we?"

He replied, "Lots of estimates." I told him what happened, and he said, "Well, you learned two things. One, you don't have a glass jaw, or it would be broken with a hit like that. Two, don't kiss other guy's girls, which I told you before."

I smiled and thanked my dad, and I gave him a hug and started for the door. As I walked away he said, "Pete." I turned as he continued, "Stop giving away my glasses I left in the house we are remodeling. I know you bring girls there, and I had 24. Now, there are 6 left. Stop giving them away as trophies. Also, I know mom promised you a car if you graduated. She hasn't stopped reminding me, so we will start looking for a car, but you must pay the insurance. Do you have any money saved?" I replied that I didn't, so he went on. "OK, when we get the car, I will take it out of your pay. Remember what I said, a fool is soon parted from his money." I smiled as I walked back to him and hugged him.

I said, "Yes that is true, but what memories he can have."

He laughed and said, "Go thank your mother, and Pete stop burning the candle at both ends; it will catch up to you."

I ran upstairs, opened the door, and saw my mother ironing our shirts. I went over hugged and kissed her while saying, "Thanks for telling Dad to get me a car."

She replied, "You're welcome. Besides he is getting tired of smelling girls' perfume in his car."

CHAPTER 13

It was the beginning of October in 1962. I took the 101st Avenue bus to my friend Charlie's house. We were going to go hang out at Cross Bay in the 1953 Mercury he had just bought. When I got on the bus, I saw a friend, Tony, and another guy, called Austin, and asked where they were going. Tony replied, "I'm going to meet some girl Judy."

"That's nice. Have a good time," I responded as the bus pulled up to my stop. I was ready to get off the bus, when I looked out the bus window and saw that Charlie's car was gone. I said to Tony, "Mind if I tag along?"

Tony said, "OK, but she's not a looker."

"That's OK. I just wanted to kill some time."

We had to transfer from the 101st Avenue bus to the Sutphin Boulevard bus. As the bus headed south, I asked Tony why we were heading into an all-Black neighborhood. I said, "While I have no preference, what color is this girl?"

Tony laughed and said, "There is a small group of Pollocks and a few Italians that still live there."

The bus stopped at 110th Avenue, and we got off. There was an empty lot and a row of buildings with stores on the bottom and apartments on top. We walked past a few buildings and stopped in front of one. Tony rang the bell and then looked up. This prompted the rest of us to look up, and that is the first time I met Judy's mother, Mrs. Gertrude Lampicky. She came to the window and looked down at us. Tony asked her if Judy was coming out. Mrs. Lampicky said she would tell her we were here and we should wait in the hallway until she came down because it was cold out. We entered the hallway and waited at the bottom of the steps, standing there and having small talk. I heard the door open and saw Judy come out.

To me, the day seems like it was yesterday. Judy came down the steps slowly; she was smiling, and even in the dark hallway you could see her pearl-white teeth, her Coppertone tan, her red hair in curlers, and her beautiful face. This is saying nothing of her knockout body. She was wearing black ski pants with a lighter black mohair sweater showing her perfect curves. Tony introduced us, and we all stood at the bottom of the steps in the dim lights, talking and getting to know each other. Eventually, she said it was late and she would have to go. "Pleasure meeting you, Pete, Austin. See you Tony." Then she turned around and walked up the steps. We watched her go up the steps and into her apartment, a view well worth watching. When we returned back home, I thanked Tony and Austin and offered to buy them a drink, but they declined.

I was doing what I do best, burning the candle at both ends. I didn't think about Judy. I was busy trying to keep three girls happy. First, there was Lisa, a Russian that modeled bras for Sears, and, believe me, they looked better out than in. Then there was Marylin, an airline stewardess, who said we could participate in other sexual activities, but not intercourse. (That is another story.) Finally, I had Susan, a manager for a large department store, who kept giving me various men colognes. My father was putting the clamp on my use of the car. This was probably because the car smelled of perfume and sex, I never put gas in, and I gave away his airline drinking glasses every time I scored with a girl at the house we were working on. But I was holding my own.

One day in November, I was sitting in Grace's Ice Cream Shop listening to "She Cried" on the juke box. I was also listening to Lester talk about robbing a bank when Tony came in and said, "Pete, Judy would like to date you, and she gave me her telephone number."

I smiled and said, "Me?"

Tony said, "Yep."

I said, "Thanks Tony."

Then Lester asked, "Who is Judy?"

"None of your business. You have Donna," I replied. I went to the phone booth and called Judy. She answered, and I asked if she would like to go out with me to celebrate my birthday. I told her that I would be picking her up in my father's Cadillac. What I did not tell her was that the Cadillac was a beat-up 1952 one. She agreed to the date, so I said, "Great, pick you up about 5:30."

She was waiting for me in front of her building, and when I saw her, my heart was in my throat. I was looking at the most beautiful young girl I had ever seen. I pulled up, and she gave me a look of surprise but did not say anything. Her mother was at the front window, so I introduced myself. She said, "Hello." I then helped Judy into the car, and we started for the movies. She told me that her father said she had to be home at 12, no later. While watching the movie, we kissed, but I did not make any moves.

On the way to her house, the car got a flat, so I got out and fixed it. Unfortunately, I got her home about 12:15. I walked her up the steps and to the front door. Her father opened the door and angrily informed us that we were late. Judy tried to explain, but he told her get inside and shut the door. He stood there looking at me, and while apologizing, I put my hands out, showing him my dirty hands and explaining to him about the flat. While talking, I noticed that we stood the same height, except he was solid muscle. I later found out that he worked as a longshoreman, which account for his muscular body. After listening to my explanation, he said, "OK, never let it happen again."

"Yes sir," I affirmed; then I left. That night was the beginning of a long, rocky relationship.

The next time I saw Judy, I was driving a beautiful baby blue 1958 Oldsmobile convertible that my parents had helped me buy. My father was worried about it being a convertible, as it had no roof protection in case I had an accident and the car rolled over. I promised him I wouldn't have an accident, but he just sadly looked at me and said, "I hope so."

As our relationship progressed, I would pick Judy up after work, and we would go out to various places. When we would see our friends, we would introduce each other. I was told more than once that I was a lucky bastard. The biggest problem was she would not let me touch her inappropriately when we were making out, and when my hand would roam, she would gently move my hand and say, "No." This was causing me to take cold showers and search for girls that would let my hands roam. We went through this routine for over a year, breaking up then making up.

CHAPTER 14

It was a clear morning. The road looked clear, so I put the pedal to the metal. The speedometer was rising to 90 when I noticed the hood of my car crumble inward and come toward me. The next thing I remember is hearing someone say, "Is he dead?" Sirens were blaring in the background. I was rushed to Mary Immaculate Hospital. I was soon released and sent home. That same night, I woke up choking on my own blood. My mother heard me and came into my room, only to find me choking on my blood. She screamed and fainted – some things never change. My father came in, stood me up, put towels under my mouth, and rushed me to the hospital. That is the last thing I remember.

I woke up to see my mother and Judy, crying as the priest performed my last rites. The palate of my mouth was split open. The doctors tried everything, but they could not stop the bleeding, so I was bleeding to death. Now this is where my mother believes an angel was sent to save me. The doctors were around my bed, trying to figure out how to stop the bleeding. Suddenly, an unknown doctor came from behind and said, "Didn't anyone hear of direct pressure?" He took a piece of gauze, put it over the crack that was in the palate of my mouth, and told the nurses to keep pressure on the wound for 24 hrs. They were to change nurses every 10 minutes. As quickly as he showed up, he left. My mother says no one knew who he was.

After a couple of weeks, I was released from the hospital. I looked like a walking skeleton with skin on it. I was told not to bend or to lift anything, even an empty pail, for two months, and I had to go to Queen's General Hospital Hematology department once a week. There they would take blood from me because the marrow of my bone was still making blood even though the bleeding had stopped.

Judy would take the bus to see me, but I was a miserable bastard, and as a result, we started to drift apart. Since we never said were going steady or said that we loved each other, other guys were looking to date her, but I made sure no one knew where she lived. However, one day her father took his car to a garage, where a mechanic saw her and asked her out. From that moment they started to date. As for me, I had plenty female company; my sister's friends were always in my house, for one reason or another, waiting for me to ask them out. When I wasn't around girls at home, I'd go to the bar where there was no shortage of them.

I knew I was getting better because I started to gain weight and get my looks back. Finally, I was able to go to work. I asked my father for a loan, to be taken out of my pay. He agreed, and I bought a 1957 gray Oldsmobile with white roll and pleated interior. It had been about two months since I had seen Judy, so I drove over to her house and waited for her to walk her dog, which she did routinely every night at about 7. Judy walked past the car and was looking away from me when I walked up behind her and said, "Hello Judy." She turned quickly, and when she saw me, her face lit up.

She said my name, and I grabbed her close to me and kissed her. Our kiss lasted for a while; then she pulled back and said, "I'm still mad at you."

I replied, "Let me make it up to you. Let me take you out to dinner tomorrow night. I have a new car." I pointed to the Oldsmobile.

She smiled and said, "That is a nice car, but I can't go out with you. I have a date."

"OK, some other time," I responded and started to walk away.

I heard her say, "I'm free Sunday and every day after that."

I said, "Great! See you at about 2 on Sunday."

She smiled and said, "OK."

CHAPTER 15

I drove to the Imperial Bar, walked in, and saw some friends sitting at a table. I headed over to the table and sat down, saying, "What's up?"

Lester said, "I'm still planning to rob the First National Bank. Want in?"

I said, "No thanks. By the way, my neighbor across the street was telling my father that someone with a big pair of balls stole the engine and tranny out of his new car in the middle of the night." Smiling, I continued, "Didn't you say you needed an engine?"

Lester looked at me and said, "What a coincidence, I just got a new engine." We laughed, then I finished my drink and got up, reminding Lester to be careful before walking to the door. I stopped to blow a kiss to Linda, who was pole dancing on a small stage. She blew a kiss back and asked, "When are we going out?"

I replied, "Soon."

Saturday night came, and I went to the Imperial Bar; it was buzzing with life. I really felt great, which I hadn't in a long time. Marylin was in town, and when she saw me, she came right over, smiling. "Long time no see, want a drink?" she asked. "At my place?"

I said, "Sure, let's go."

We started drinking heavily, and while making out, we started to get undressed. There is nothing like seeing a pretty, completely naked girl lying before you. It was a good thing that I was drunk, or I would have climaxed right there. She pulled me forward and started kissing me, as I entered her. But it didn't feel good; it was like sticking my manhood in the air. There was no feeling, nothing. She smiled and said, "I told you not to try sex that way. Now lay back, and I will take care of you." I leaned back, looking at her as she admired my 9-and-½-inch manhood. She was about to give me oral sex, when the door opened and Lester walked in

He said, "Hi Sis. Hi Wolfie." Then he kept walking into the bedroom.

I said, "Lester is your brother?"

She replied, "Yep," and went back to trying to make me happy.

I stopped her and said, "I'm not in the mood." I started to get dressed.

She asked, "What's the problem?"

I said, "Nothing," got dressed, and gave her a long kiss before going out of the door.

It was Sunday. I got up, and my head was killing me. I didn't remember where I parked my car, so I gave my brother, Charlie, a dollar to find it, hoping I didn't hit anything. He found it parked around the corner on the sidewalk with the keys still in it. I got to Judy's at about 2:15. When she came down, she looked at me and asked, "Are you all right? You look pale." She bent over to kiss me, and I told her I was fine. She inquired, somewhat judgmentally, "You weren't drinking were you? You know you just got over a bad accident."

I said, "No. It must have been something I ate." I pulled out from the curb and started driving. I made a right-hand turn down a street I normally don't go down, and Judy said, "Stop! Please go some other way." When I asked why, she said, "Because I had a dream that we saw a crowd in the street, and when we went through the crowd, we saw someone dead." I laughed and continued to drive. Suddenly, we heard screeching tires ahead, and then we saw a big crowd in the street. I got out to walk through the crowd and saw a little boy lying on the street. I turned around, got back into the car, and looked at Judy, saying, "How did you know?"

She replied, "I have no idea. I have a dream or feeling about something, and it just happens. My mother calls me a witch."

We went to the movies. As I dropped her off, I said, "There is a Moose dance next Saturday, do you want to go?"

She smiled and said, "Yes!"

I replied, "Good, I will see you at about 5. I have to get flowers for Grandmother; it is her anniversary."

Even though I saw Judy every night for a few minutes when she walked her dog, I had to tell her ahead of time about any dances. She needed time; I learned that the hard way.

I picked Judy up, and we headed for the florist first to get flowers before going to the dance. I couldn't find a parking space in front of the store, so I parked around the block, got out, went and got the flowers, and was getting back into the car when I noticed a young woman sitting on the stoop across the street, minding some small children. I told Judy I'd be right back; I was going to see an old friend.

I walked across the street and stood in front of the young woman She was playing with a young child, and when I approached, she looked up. She smiled and said, "Pete, how have you been?"

I replied, "Fine, and you?"

She said, "Good." She caught me looking at the older child and said, "Don't go there."

"I won't," I promised. "It looks like you been busy, Eleanor." She ignored my remark and asked if the beautiful woman in the car was my wife. I said, "Maybe someday. I have to go, or we will be late for a dance. It's been good seeing you again, Eleanor."

She replied, "Same here."

I got into the car and started to drive away, smiling. Judy said, "Who was she? And why are you smiling?"

I told her, "She is just an old friend, and I'm happy." (I was thinking my father was right; time heals all wounds. I actually saw her and spoke to her, and my heart did not hurt.) I looked at Judy and said to myself, "Life is great."

CHAPTER 16

Life was back to normal: I would go out with Judy, my hands would roam, and she would stop them and kiss me. We went out one night, and Judy kept looking at the rear side of my car. When I asked why, she said, "I have a feeling that the car will be hit right there."

I laughed and said, "Don't worry." We went to the movies; then I dropped her off at home. I headed home myself because I had to work the next day and my father wanted an early start. The next morning, as I entered the shop, I noticed my car on the sidewalk. I know I didn't put it there, so I walked over and noticed that someone hit it the night before, right where Judy said it would be. The hit totaled the car. I called Judy and told her what had happened. I then said, "Never tell me anything like that again." I went to my father and asked for another loan for a car.

He said, "OK, but you will have nothing left in your pay if you don't work a full week." I agreed and bought a 1959 two-door Oldsmobile hardtop.

My life was back to the routine: work, Judy, nightlife, sleep, and work. One night after I dropped Judy off and promised to go straight home because she said I looked pale, I stopped at the bar. (Judy should have known that I was burning the candle at both ends because of her not allowing my hands to roam.) I saw Charlie, Joe, and his girl, Terry, when I walked in. When they saw me, Charlie asked if I wanted to go to Rockaway and walk along the boardwalk. I said, "Sure, why not?"

Charlie was making a turn onto the main street, so we could park. The turn was close to a group of Black people who were about to cross the street.

The group started cursing us out loud, but we didn't pay attention and parked the car. We got out and were ready to cross the street and go onto the boardwalk when we heard a lot of screaming and cursing. We turned to see the group running toward us. Charlie went to his car trunk and opened it up. I was looking at the group approaching us and said, "Just said pass me the tire bar."

Then I heard Charlie say, "The next spook that takes another step is a dead spook." I turned and looked to see Charlie holding a rifle, and he had it pointed right at them. They all turned and ran away.

Joe said to Charlie, "We better get out of here."

Charlie responded, "Why? The rifle is legal; I use it for hunting." He no sooner finished saying that when a cop car pulled up. The officers got out and asked us to put our hands up in the air. They informed us that they had received a complaint that a white male and his friends were threating a group of Black people with a weapon.

We explained what happened. The white cop wanted to let us go, but the Black cop refused. So we were taken to the Rockaway Station. While we were being booked, I told the desk sergeant that I just met the other guys, and they were giving me a lift home. I stated that I had just left my girlfriend's house and said, "If you call her, she will verify that I just left her house." The desk sergeant called Judy, but Judy said she had never heard of me, so the sergeant said, "Lock them up, except for the girl. Her parents are coming to get her."

After a few hours, the cops came back to our cells and told us that they were only keeping Charlie, because he pointed the gun. I asked the sergeant to call my father to ask if he would come and get me. The sergeant called, smiled, and hung up, saying, "Your father said you got yourself there, get yourself back." Joe and I were lucky to hitch a ride to 101st Avenue, where we were then able to take a bus home.

The next day I called Judy, but her mother said she didn't want to talk to me. I drove over to house and waited outside until she walked the dog. When she saw me, she turned her back. I walked over to her and apologized; she turned, looked up at me, and said, "I'm tired of your wildness and foolishness. I don't think we should see each other anymore."

I begged, "Come on, Judy. Give me another chance."

She turned back to look at me and said, "No." Then she walked away crying. I went back home, ran up to my bed, and lay down. My mother panicked, seeing me home early and in bed, I heard her holler down the airshaft to my father to come upstairs because she thought something was wrong with me.

My father came into my room and asked, "What is wrong? Are you OK?"

I told him that Judy had broken up with me. He replied, "She is getting you ready for marriage. She loves you."

I said, "She doesn't show it."

"Son, I'm telling you as a father and man, Judy is an extremely beautiful young woman. When you take her to the Moose and oil burner dances, men, boys, young, old, single, or married look at Judy. But she never looks back at them or looks around. Her eyes are only on you, and son I love you, but better-looking guys than you looked at her, and her eyes never left you. Now, let's see how you match up to her loyalty. You almost killed yourself racing. You drink, gamble, go to the bar, never have any money, and are always in debt. On top of that, you have various girls hanging out when she comes up here."

I tried to defend myself, saying, "Hey, they are my sister's friends."

My father responded, "I know for a fact that you dated every one of them at least once, and they are up here waiting for another date. And I'm sure you notice men looking at Judy."

I said, "I do, but I remember what you said when Eleanor and I broke up: 'You cannot keep a woman if she does not want be with you.'"

My father said, "That does not apply to Judy. You are the one that is breaking all the rules, but, son, it is up to you: Change or lose her." He got up, told my mother I was OK, and when back downstairs.

I lay there in bed thinking about what my father said; for an old man he was pretty smart. I said to myself, "I never told anyone where Judy lived, so I don't think I'll have much competition. I'll give her a few days to cool off, then I'll ask her to speak to me."

CHAPTER 17

A week went by when I ran into my friend Johnny. I said, "Hi John." He looked a little nervous when he greeted me. I said, "Everything OK, John?"

John replied, "Pete I don't want you to get mad at me, but Tom found out you and Judy broke up, so he took her out."

I asked, "How did he find out where she lived?"

"He was over my house, and he was taking to my dad. My dad told him that he delivers the laundry to her house."

I said, "OK, where does he live?"

"Why? What are you going to do?"

I said, "Nothing. I learned the hard way, a long time ago, if a woman does not want to be with you, you cannot keep her. I just want to lay down some ground rules. After all, I still care about her."

We had just gotten to Tom's house when Tom pulled up. He got out of his car and started walking to his house, but he saw us. He said, "Hi, John." When he saw me, he stood up a little straighter and said, "Hi."

I walked up to him, and once we were standing face to face, I said, "Tom, I know you are dating Judy, and I don't have a problem with that, but treat her like a lady, or there with be problems."

Tom said, "I gave to her what I wanted, and she enjoyed it." I immediately hit him with an upper cut, sending him to the ground. Then, I stood over him, picked him up by his shirt, and gave him a few shots in the face before his father came running out of the house, screaming at me to leave him alone. Johnny grabbed my arm and said, "Let's go." When we got to Grace's Ice Cream Parlor, I went straight to the phone booth and called Judy.

She picked up the phone, so I said, "I just spoke to your boyfriend, Tom, and he told me what you and he did. You fucking slut! You won't let me touch you, but you let him? Fuck you, you little whore!" As soon as I finished, I hung up. When I stepped out of the phone booth, everyone was staring out me. I asked, "What, nobody here never heard a curse?" I walked out the door and drove to the Imperial Bar, saying to myself, "Boy was my father wrong on that one."

A few weeks went by, and I ran into Lester at the Imperial Bar. We started talking about this and that when he said, "Boy does Judy have some temper."

I said, "What, you've seen her?"

He replied, "Yeah, I saw her walking on 101st Avenue, so I pulled over and asked if she wanted a lift. She said, 'OK, I'm headed home.' On the way she told me what happened. She was so mad. She took three buses to that guy's house, and when he answered the door, she smacked him in the face, told him off, and left."

I sat there stunned, all I could say was, "Did you give her a lift in the car with the stolen engine?"

He laughed and said, "Yeah, who is going to look under the hood?"

That the night I waited for Judy to walk the dog. When she saw me, she turned her back to me. I walked up to her and said, "Judy, please turn around and talk to me."

She wouldn't, so I gently turned her toward me. She looked up at me, and I could see the tears coming down her face. I said, "Judy, I'm truly sorry for what I said. I was mad and hurt." I gently pulled her toward me and put my arms around her as she laid the side of her head on my chest. I could feel her crying from her heart, making my heart break for my stupidity.

Eventually, she said, "You hurt me, Pete, really hurt me. Not only for what you called me, but what you think I would allow him to do to me." She looked up at me, continuing, "I love you and won't let you touch me. Why would you think I would let anyone else touch me?"

I looked at her and said, "I love you too, and I promise if you give me another chance, I will never hurt you again. I will try very hard to be good. No racing, gambling, drinking, whore chasing." While in my mind, I said, "I will only do those things when really needed."

She was happy, and I was just happy to have her back. I asked her once why the no touch, and she replied, "I believe I should be a virgin when we marry. I also saw my girlfriend, Ann, get hurt by a guy after giving herself to him. Believe me, I did want to give in a few times for you, but I was scared, and I believe it was wrong." I really didn't have a comeback, so I waited.

CHAPTER 18

On my 21st birthday I asked Judy to marry me, and she said, "Yes." Life was great. I took all of the city exam tests for city jobs, and Judy and I planned to marry in 7 months, on June 19,1966. When I could, I would pick her up from work and take her home. She said I didn't have to, but her girlfriend said that when she waited for the bus men were always making remarks about her figure and beauty. She would get mad and upset and tell them off. It was hard for Judy in a lot of ways. She always saw herself as just a pretty girl and never thought different. She always wore nice clothes, but when she wore them, they looked sexy. I guess it was hard to hide a 36"-24"-36" figure.

One day she got in the car upset, and I asked her what was wrong. Thinking someone said something about her beauty or figure, I was surprised when she said she had had a horrible dream. She explained, "I saw a green snake wrap around you and take you away from me."

I laughed and said, "Don't worry. It was just a dream." However, three days later, I received a letter to report to Whitehall Street for a physical. I didn't tell Judy; I did not want to worry her.

When I got to Whitehall Street, it seemed like my whole neighborhood was there. The doctor examined me and asked why I was a 1Y. I explained that I had a car accident and split the pallet of my mouth. He looked into my mouth and said, "Yes, I see the scar. It healed nicely." He quietly finished the rest of the exam, then I left.

A week later I received a letter in the mail stating that I was drafted and had to report to Fort Dix at 08:00 a.m. on June 19, 1966. That was our planned wedding day. My time to report was about a month away, so I told my family. Everyone was upset, especially my grandmother, because we had lost my cousin, Ronnie, about a month before. The hardest part was telling Judy. When I told her, she went white and started crying. I held her, not knowing what to say, except, "Everything will be OK."

We canceled all our wedding plans, went to the priest, and asked if we could get married sooner. He said, "Pete, there is always a chance you may not come home. Do really want to take that chance, knowing that the woman you love may be with child and left alone?"

I said, "No."

As we left the church, Judy looked mad, so I asked, "What's the matter?"

Judy said, "He should have asked me."

I responded, "And what would you have said?"

She replied, "I would have said yes, I still want to marry him." I took her in my arms and looked at her. I could see the sadness in her eyes, so I bent down and right before our lips met said, "That is why he asked me."

The next morning, my father said to me, "Come with me." I asked where we were going, but he replied, "Just come with me." Before I knew it, we were standing in front of a congressman's office.

My father walked in and informed the secretary that the congressman was waiting for him. The secretary replied, "Go right in."

Once in the office, the man said, "Hello, Charlie, please sit down, and how can I help you?"

My father replied, "My son is being drafted. His grandmother is very upset; we have lost one already, and she is afraid that she will lose another. Pat [he is a big time bookie and grew up with my father], our friend, said you might be able to help us." I sat there in shock, my father kept talking about his mother being afraid of losing me.

Eventually, the congressman said, "I could use a new bathroom."

My father consented, "Whatever you want."

The congressman said, "Well, I could keep him stateside for a little more than a year, then he will be too short of time in the military to go overseas. How does that sound?" He looked at my father then me.

I said, "Thank you, but no thank you." I then went to get up, but my father grabbed my arm and said, "Please Pete, we are worried about you. My mother, your grandmother, is extremely worried about you." This was first time I had ever seen my father about to cry.

I said, "Dad you took your chances, and I will take mine." The congressman stood up, handed my father and me a card, and said, "Call anytime, and I will arrange everything." I put the card in my wallet and left. When we got downstairs, I thought my father was going to hit me; he was so angry and sad. He walked away, and we never spoke about it again. I kept that card in my wallet for 11 months and 29 days while I was over in Vietnam. I would be lying if I said I didn't think about calling.

The following week, I said all my goodbyes to my loved ones. My father offered to take me to Fort Dix with my brother Charlie. On the way, we stopped at a diner that was about 10 minutes from Fort Dix. As we were having coffee, my father said, "Do you know that this road goes straight to Canada?"

I could see the worried look on his face as he said that. Looking at my brother and then my father I smiled and said, "I know. I planned on taking Judy there someday." We arrived in the parking lot 10 minutes later and said our goodbyes before I walked through the gate to join the largest gang in the world, the United States Army.

CHAPTER 19

We arrived at Fort Gordon, which is in Augusta, Georgia, for basic training. It was a new way of life. In boot camp, they would break you down and then build you up, teaching you how to kill and be a member of the team.

I was homesick the first few weeks, like everyone else. We were allowed to write, but there were no phone calls. I received a letter from my father with twenty dollars in it; he wrote the following:

Dear Son:

You are probably sitting on your bunk broke and reading this letter [I said to myself, "He is a mind reader"], *enclosed is 20 dollars, use it wisely, buy razors, soap, movie tickets, make it stretch till next pay day, this is the last one you will get.*

Love
Dad

I did what he said, except for the movies; you never had enough free time for the movies. The hardest time for me was at night when I was lying in bed; I always got homesick and missed Judy.

The sergeants were hard on you, and sometimes you would think they were the enemy.

Right before target practice, you would stand while holding your rifle and say, "This is a rifle made to kill." Then you would grab your manhood and say, "This is a gun made for fun." They would make you repeat it until the range was ready. I did well and earned the expert badge, which also gave me a weekend day pass. The six of us who earned passes stood before the Sergeant as he gave them out. He recommended that we stay on base. Of course, no one listened, and we headed for town, which was right outside the gates. Once outside, the two Black guys in our group said, "See you." When we asked why they were going a different way, they said, "We are going to the Black part of town."

Doc, who was a real hick, said he was told that the hotel had a prostitute there, and she charged 30 dollars. One guy said, "Not for me," and went his own way, which left three of us. We were given the hotel room, and we all went up and knocked on the door. A nice-looking woman, about 40, opened the door wearing negligee. The guy who wanted to be called "Ace" said, "I'm here for you."

"Come right on in," she said while turning to us and saying, "You can come in if you want." We declined and make plans to meet him back at camp.

Doc and I were walking, looking in the store window. I could not believe you could walk into a store and just by a gun. While we were walking, a Black lady carrying what looked like two heavy bags of groceries was walking toward us, so I stepped into the street so she could pass. Doc looked at me in shock. I stepped back on the sidewalk, then I felt a hand grab me by my collar, throwing me up against a wall. I was spun around by a big heavyset sheriff, who was staring me in the face. He said, "You think you're smart, boy?" He was shaking me.

I said, "What do you mean?" Not knowing what I did wrong. I heard my friend Doc say to the sheriff, "He don't know what he did, boss man."

The sheriff stopped shaking me and looked at him. He said, "Where you from boy?"

Doc said, "I'm from Hollow Stick."

The sheriff said, "Why you with this Yankee?"

Doc replied, "He's my friend. He doesn't know no better."

The sheriff let me go and said, "You're lucky, boy," before walking away. I ask Doc what I did wrong.

He pointed to two drinking fountains with signs that said "white only" and "colored only." I said, "This is 1966, and they're still fighting the Civil War. Hell, I'm going back to base."

That night I called Judy. It was cheaper at night, and it was the first time I spoke to her since I left. We told each other how much we loved each other and what was happening. Before we knew it, my 10 dollars in coin was used up.

CHAPTER 20

The standard basic training is 10 weeks, but our training was 14 weeks long. We went into boot camp not knowing we had four weeks more than the standard because we were being trained for infantry and armor. Two weeks before my company was to finish, half of us got pneumonia. They said it was because we were from the North, and we were not used to the Southern climate. I think it was because we did a forced 10-mile hike in the pouring rain and then stood for an hour in the rain before being released to the barracks. When we were released from the hospital, we were separated and sent to different companies that had two weeks left.

It felt great to graduate. My original orders for armor were canceled and changed to be trained as a boat operator in Fort Story, Virginia. Because I had been sick, I wasn't able to start the armor class. I was not sure what a boat operator was, but I didn't care. I just wanted to see Judy. We were packed and ready to leave when the sergeant came in and started to give out our orders while saying all leaves were canceled. We were told that the buses outside were numbered. We were to look at our packages, which told us what number bus we were supposed to get on. "One peep out of anyone, and I will put my boot up your ass. You're in the army not the Girl Scouts, now move out," declared the sergeant.

I sat in the bus, thinking about what had just happened. While looking around, I could see the guys curse, cry, and talk out loud to themselves. Suddenly, I felt a pull on my sleeve; I turned to see a young, freckle-faced kid looking at me. I said, "What?"

He replied, "Aren't we lucky? The recruiter said if I sign for four more years, he would get me into this class, so I signed. How many years did you sign?"

I said, "A lot."

It was about a 4-5-hour trip to Fort Story, and we arrived late in the afternoon. A sergeant, named Rash, told us where the barracks, the chow hall, and the building and room where we were to be at 0800 for our classes were. Then he dismissed us.

The next day we sat in class, waiting for the sarge to come in. When he came in, we all stood up at attention. He smiled and said, "I'm not an officer. Sit." He stood before us, looking trim, and said, "This is a class of 40, but in less than two weeks, more than half will wash out. By the fourth week, I expect to see about 12 to 15 graduate. Any questions?"

Someone raised his hand and said, "What happens to those who wash out?"

Sarge's eyes got very small, and his face became mean-looking. He said, "Fail and find out." I thought the guy was going to shit his pants. The sarge continued, "You are going to be trained on various type of vessels, and by the time you graduate. You will be able to drive any vessel up to 20 tons. You are to be trained on amphibious craft, meaning a craft that can go from water to land, also known as a lark. You will be able to plot courses on your sea charts. You will be responsible for your vessel, as well as be in command of your vessel. Your vessel is 55 feet long and has two 300 horse Cummins diesels. You are to learn everything about your vessel. Now let's start."

Sarge was right, by the second week half our class was gone. They would be called out of class, and when we got back to the barracks, they were gone. By the fourth week, we were down to 10; the hardest part of the test was to plot a route to take the lark up a ramp into an LCU boat using only a shiny belt buckle on the sarge as a point of reference for the LCU. By the end, nine of us made it. One guy slid off the ramp, flipping the lark into the water. He got out, but the lark sank. They pulled him out of the water and took him back to base. When we got back, he was gone, and no one asked where he went. The following morning, we stood at attention as the sarge handed us each our diploma, congratulating us while stating that Dave and I were the top of our class. He then went on, calling out our names and telling us where our next assignments would be. As I was standing there, I heard Korea, Germany, and Japan. When he called my name, he said, "'Nam," then he called Dave and said, "'Nam." We were then dismissed. I walked over to the sarge and asked, "Why me and Dave?"

He said, "I'm leaving tomorrow for 'Nam, and I only want the best."

I replied, "But Sarge, I wanted to get married.

He replied, "If she loves you, she'll wait. So, you better move; you only got seven days." He turned and walked away. While packing our duffel bags, I said to Dave, "What are you doing with your seven days?"

He said, "I might go home and remarry my wife. She's a Seminole Indian, and I have nothing better to do."

I threw my bag over my shoulder and said, "Great! Enjoy yourself. See you in seven days."

CHAPTER 21

When I got home, my mother said, "I'm glad you're home; go around the corner. Mr. Lee is selling his house, and he wants to sell to you." The house was an old farmhouse that had the most property on the block. My grandfather offered to go with me, so I put my bag down and went around the corner. When we got to the house, there were about 20 people all trying to get Mr. Lee to sell to them. I entered the house, and Mr. Lee's face lit up. He said, "Pete, I'm glad you came. Do you still want to buy the house?"

I said, "Sure, but I don't think I can afford it."

Mr. Lee replied, "Remember how we sat in front of the fire place when you were a boy, and we would talk about how you loved this house? And I said 'when you are old enough, I would sell you this house for 11,000 dollars'?"

I said, "I do."

Mr. Lee stuck out his hand and said, "If you still want it, it is yours for 11,000 dollars." As I shook his hand, people started yelling at him and calling him a fool. He simply turned to them and said, "Get out of Peter's house now."

My grandfather gave Mr. Lee a $100.00 deposit. I thanked him and asked if I could bring my future wife to see the house. He said that would be fine, but that his lawyer would take care of everything because he was leaving that day. He gave me his lawyer's card and the keys, hugged me, and left.

We went back to the shop, and my father was there waiting for us. He said, "Let's go, we don't have much time." I asked where we were headed, and he responded "To Jake, my friend the lawyer." Before I knew it, we were sitting at his table. The plan was that my father would have power of attorney, and the mortgage would be in his name until I came home. The house would be rented out, using the rent money to pay the mortgage. I couldn't wait to tell Judy. I called her and told her I had a surprise for her. I drove over, picked her up, and brought her to the house while explaining everything that had happened. When we got to the house, she looked and said, "I don't want to go in." I asked why, and she replied, "Because we are not married. It is your house, not ours."

I said, "I don't understand; it is our house."

She just said, "Let's wait until we are married, then I will look at it." I stopped by the shop, gave the keys to my father, and said, "Thank you. She loved the house." I left and never said anymore about what happened or went to the house.

The time went fast. Before I knew it, it was the night before I had to leave. Judy and I sat in the car, making out. I slowly moved my hand to her breast, and she tensed a little, but to my surprise, she let my hand stay. She looked up at me and said, "You may have me if you want." I looked at her, surprised, before asking her if she was sure. She couldn't speak; she just shook her head "yes." I said to myself, "Now I know how Adam felt when Eve offered him the apple." Her breast felt firm but soft, yet I couldn't get what the priest said out of my mind. I dropped my hand, and said, "Judy, I love you with all my heart, and I want you very badly, but not this way, in a car, half undressed. We waited this long, so we can wait a little longer." Her body relaxed, and she kissed me, saying, "I love you with all my heart, and I will wait for you forever."

I smiled and said, "Let's hope it is not that long." I gently brought her close to me, and she laid her head on my chest, softly crying, I picked up her chin, seeing the love in her eyes for me. I said, "See the moon? No matter where I am, whenever you look up and see the moon, know that I will be looking at the moon thinking of you." Then I kissed her.

My father and Charlie offered to drive me to Fort Dix again, so the morning I was to leave they patiently waited for me. It took a long time to say goodbye to my mother and my grandparents. I felt bad that I was unable to say goodbye to my brother, Glen, and sister, Joanne, but they weren't able to be there. While driving, my father said, "Maybe I should keep your car and put up on blocks, so you can have it when you come home."

I said, "Thanks, Dad, but sell it. I'll buy one when I get home."

My brother Charlie said, "Don't worry, Pete. I'll have a car by then, and you could use it."

I looked at him, thinking about how big he had gotten, and said, "Thank you."

As we were driving, my father told us how his parents drove him to Fort Dix. When they got there, grandma hollered at grandpa to carry his duffel bag for him. We all laughed. I was not sure if my dad looked sad or proud. Instead of talking about the situation, I changed the subject. "Hey, Dad. I see a few gray hairs in that all black curly hair you have." He just smiled.

We pulled into the parking lot and got out. My father hugged me while saying, "Be careful."

I could see his eyes tearing. I said, "I will," as I took my duffel bag from my brother and hugged him. I walked toward the gate, but once I crossed through it, I turned and waved.

CHAPTER 22

I was put in a barracks with other guys waiting to be shipped out. I saw Dave, and he came over to me. We hugged each other, and I asked, "How was your leave?"

He smiled and said, "I got married again. And you?"

I said, "Great." Just then, the sergeant came in with a clipboard and called us all to attention. While we stood at attention, he began calling names, telling them to grab their gear, then instructed them to follow him before telling the remainder of us, "At ease."

As we stood in line waiting to board, the back of a huge cargo air craft lowered, forming a large ramp. As we walked up the ramp, we were told to put our duffel bags into what looked like a container. The bags were stacked neatly, then we proceeded forward and were marched to chairs that looked lie movie seats. Row after row we marched and sat, until all 150 of us were seated. We were told that it would take 24 hours to arrive at our destination. We would have to stop for fuel two times, and while there we would be able to stretch our legs. Dave and I made friends with a guy named Ray, who was going back for his third tour. He was a corporal, and he said that every time he goes back they give him a stripe. I asked if he had any advice, and he said, "Yeah, remember this once you set foot in Vietnam: You could be killed at any time. Anywhere. It doesn't matter what branch of military you're in or what job you have, the goal of the enemy is to kill you anyway they can. They will put acid in soda bottles, then put the cap on, so turn it over before drinking. If you want to get laid, stick your finger up there first. They have been known to put single edge razor blades up there. Trust none of them, and don't let them get close to you." By the time he got done telling us all the things that could happen to us, I was afraid to touch the chair I was sitting in. I was also thinking, *this guy is nuts to go back.*

When we landed in Saigon, they had a line of trucks waiting for us; we got on one heading to Long Bin, where we had a short stayover before moving on to our final destination Cam Ranh Bay. While we were getting our bed ready, I heard thump-thump, and someone hollered, "Mail!" At that point, holy hell broke loose. A guy stuck his head in the tent, yelling, "Put the mattress over you until you hear 'all clear.'" We all did it automatically, no questions asked. As I lay there hearing screaming, gunships, helicopters, and explosions, I said to myself, "Welcome to Vietnam."

The attack lasted about 10 minutes, and these types of short attacks, I later found out, were known as a hit and run. To me, that 10 minutes felt like 10 hours. We finally heard "All clear." I pushed the mattress and was getting up when someone entered and asked if everyone was all right. Once everyone gave the OK, he hollered, "You two with the fancy medals [expert rifle badge], get dressed in you greens now and make it quick. I'll be outside waiting."

Dave and I dug through our duffel bags and were dress in less than 5 minutes. When we came out, we were directed to the armory, where we were issued a rifle and ammo belt with spare clips. There were about 18 of us, so we lined up. The guy from earlier was there, and he said, "When we leave the compound, flank across the field, shoot anything in front of you, watch where you walk, and if you see something, stop and raise your hand. Touch nothing. Safety off. Now, move out."

As I was walking in the knee-high grass, I could hear the gunships going back and forth. We'd walked the length of a football field when I heard, "Halt, about face, forward." We did the same sweep back to the compound. When we reached the compound, only the transit personnel were told to turn in their weapons. I was surprised that we did not have to clean them first.

The next day we had breakfast and got on the truck going to Cam Ranh Bay. They dropped us off in front of HQ (headquarters). The sign outside read "458 Sea Tigers." We went in and said, "Reporting for duty." Sergeant Rash turned when he heard our voices, smiled, and said, "What took you so long?" Turning to a private, he said, "Show them their tents. Today is your last day of rest. Tomorrow you work."

We entered our tent and saw about six cots on each side. The private said, "Grab an empty cot." Then he left. This tent was our home for 11 months and 29 days. Our main job was to move explosives from ship to shore, then from the shore to various ammo dumps. I was assigned number 246. A five-ton lark is 55 feet long and has two 300 Cummins diesel engines. We were fully responsible for our boat. Once I set foot on my boat, I was totally in command. I could tell of many incidents that happened to me while there, but I would not want to bore you or scare you. I will, however, tell you of a few.

CHAPTER 23

It was around August 1967. Sergeant Rash had sent for me, so I went into his office and shut the door. He said, "Pete, I want you to go out to troop ship 428." He showed me the location on the sea chart stand. He continued, "Wait for orders, then bring them back to me. The ship is located about 3 miles out in the South China Sea. Fill the fuel tanks to the top. Tell no one where you are going. Stay in the center of the bay. (Cam Ranh Bay is 20 miles long and 10 miles wide.) There is to be no radio contact unless it is necessary, understand necessary."

I said, "Yes, Sarge. Who should I take?"

He replied, "Take Bob." (Bob had a PhD and did not believe in God.)

I asked, "Sarge, why him?

Sarge said, "He is expendable." Before I could say anything, he said, "You have a lucky horse shoe up your ass [a fact that was known from previous incidents]."

I went and got Bob, and we did the final check before moving out. Bob kept asking where we were going. I simply told him, "For a ride." We reached the ship, and I moored to the gang walkway. I told the officer on deck what I was there for, and he said, "Stand by."

It was a beautiful day, and Bob kept telling how he was going to prove there is no God. He firmly believed he would find the last gas in the universe and use that to prove there is no God. At one time, he thought he had found it, but he was wrong. I told him, "That's because God was fucking with you." It was about noon when we smelled food, and, being hungry, I asked the guys on the ship for a few sandwiches. They sent down two roast beef sandwiches and two Cokes. I can still taste that roast beef. We were just finished when my radio clicked on, saying all small boats were to report back to base immediately as there was a severe storm moving in. I called up to the officer on deck and said we had to go because a storm was coming in. He went someplace and came back saying, "Stand by."

I said to Bob, "Let's check everything and make sure everything is secure, all hatches are tight, and let's put on our life jackets." I could see Bob was getting nervous. Because of his personality, not many men would work with him, so he didn't spend much time on vessels. Plus, he preferred, not to be on one.

Finally, the officer of the day came running down the gang walkway, actually apologizing as he handed me the sealed container. I thanked him, saluted, and then went to my wheel. As Bob was untiring our lines, I said to myself, "That is rare, when an officer says he is sorry." I took a long last look at my chart, got my headings, and started in. The first sign of trouble was when we stopped seeing birds. I ordered Bob to strap in; he knew something was wrong. I opened the engines up and started moving fast. The water looked like glass, then large rain drops came down, making large circles in the water. The water's surface looked like it was covered in thousands of lily pads. The waves started to pick up, becoming choppy. Then large waves were forming. We kept moving, but it felt like we were standing still. The waves were getting larger, to the point where we couldn't see the crest; the waves would crash down on our bow, pushing us down under the water only for us to pop up thank to the big balloon tires. Bob started screaming that we were going to die, and he started asking God to save us. He was loudly declaring all his thoughts, but I couldn't hear much over the roar of the wind and water. I did, however, hear him praying to God. To be honest, I was getting scared myself; I was afraid that the large waves would flip us backward, and my compass was spinning like a yo-yo. It was dark. I wasn't sure if I was going or coming; I was afraid my bow was going to crack from hitting the waves so hard. (Since I happened to have so many close calls, I believed that when God called me home I was going to know and I was going to go.) It did cross my mind that God might be calling me home right then, but I started to see a glimpse of land through the heavy rains.

My next problem was determining which side was the enemy's and which side was ours. The waves started to get smaller though the rain was still heavy. Finally, I saw our flag. I had never been so happy. I started to cut an angle across the bay when suddenly I hit the rocks. I knew we were safe. As we got off the boat, I noticed Sergeant Rash was standing there in the rain. He held out his hand, and I handed him the sealed container. He turned, gave it to an officer who was sitting in a jeep, saluted the officer, turned to Bob and me, and said "Good job. Go dry out. I'll have someone check your boat." I believe Bob actually smiled.

From that day forward, every time I saw Bob, I would say, "Going to church, Bob?" He would just smile, and the other guys would look at me like I was nuts.

CHAPTER 24

There was some more excitement on my patrols, but for the most part everything was quiet. I loved sitting in my boat at night, looking up at the stars. It felt like you could reach out and grab them, and when the moon was full, I would look up with an aching heart, wondering if Judy was looking too.

Things were back to as normal as could be; we would load 5 tons of explosives on our boat, then head to shore. From shore, we would head to various ammo dumps or other locations. Our camp was fairly safe, though once in a while we would get incoming. Fortunately, they never really hit our camp. Then one day everything started to change. I woke up to see John laying in his cot with blood all over him. I called to Dave and Took, "We better check John." On closer inspection, we noticed that John's throat was cut. Took ran to get the sarge, and no one said anything. We just stared at John in shocked silence.

The sarge came in; he said, "Close the flaps. Now listen very carefully, this is how we are going to say this happened. John got a 'Dear John' letter, so he cut his wrists during the night. We do not want the camp being on edge. It is extremely important that you all keep you mouths shut. At morning call I will say that John committed suicide, and because of more enemy activity, we will be increasing guards. We will change our call name every 10 hours, and everyone will be challenged by the guards, both coming and going. We will start water and land patrols; the armory will be open 24/7. If any of you say anything different, I promise you will face a court martial. Now Wolfie, get a body bag. Took, get a mop, and Dave, close up one side.

Keep everyone out on the other side. Do we understand?" We all replied that we understood, then went to do what we were told.

I started sleeping with a knife under my pillow. Took had a small revolver under his pillow, and Dave had a Bowie knife under his pillow. The hardest part was not answering all the questions the guys were asking.

A few weeks later, while unloading our vessel, I heard a shot, and the fork truck operator fell off his truck. "Everyone take cover!" ordered someone. A call went out to the gun ship, and the ground troops started returning fire. As a driver, I never carried a weapon; this was because of the explosives, just think if a weapon went off accidentally, but we always had support. A sniper narrowly missed me, and a bullet hit my windshield. Dave was sleeping between bomb crates, but he quickly woke up, cursing about the noise. He never even knew what happened. After the skirmish, we gave our report to Sarge, who politely informed me that I had a horseshoe up my ass.

He then said, "Wolfie, I'm sending you up to Nha Trang. Pick up some money before you leave tomorrow."

I asked what the money was for. He replied, "This is your first trip. The money is for the farmer who will throw his daughter under your wheels and demand money for killing her. She will be tied and gagged. Pay him the set amount, no more, then move on. There's always a chance for an ambush. Be ready to move out tomorrow at 0800. Dave, you and Took will stay here."

I asked, "What about my support?"

Sarge replied, "You will have a squad in front and back for protection."

The next day we headed out for Nha Trang and arrived without any trouble. The officer at the base told us where to unload the explosives. That night we had dinner, which was pretty good. We were relaxing when the officer came in a said, "Specialist Wolfinger here?"

I stood up and said, "Yes sir."

He replied, "Good. Come with me to headquarters." As I entered HQ, I saw a Green Beret officer standing there; the Captain came forward and introduced everyone. While turning to me, he said "Your captain said you are the person for this job." I looked puzzled, so he continued, "I'll explain. You are to take a team to this location. Here are the coordinates. When you hear three clicks on your radio, bring them in and then leave. Any questions?"

I replied, "Sir, when my vessel is in water, I have a partner or backup. Because I drove up on land, I did not take one."

The captain smiled and said, "You think you need one?"

"No sir," I replied.

The Green Beret officer said, "Good, we leave tonight at 2300 hours. Specialist Wolfinger, get some rest."

I left the meeting, and on the way out I asked the OD (officer of the day) to wake me at 2200. Then, I was taken to the guest quarters, where I would be allowed to sleep while I was there.

It felt like I had just lain down when I heard my name. I got up and thanked the OD while checking my boots for any uninvited guest. Then, I used the latrine to put water on my face in order to bring myself back to life. I walked down to my vessel and performed one more final check. The cabin was open in the rear, and all my gauges were lit in red. I was looking for some rope when I heard my name called, so I went to the edge of my vessel and looked down. I saw three men before me. I said, "Wolfinger here. Welcome aboard." The men climbed up, and we introduced ourselves to each other.

One said, "Red lights? Where are the girls?"

I replied, "They saw you coming, so they left." We all laughed; then, I started the engines and slowly entered the water. As we headed out to sea, there was no moon, only stars. We arrived at our destination, and I stopped the engines and said, "I was told to wait here till 0100."

One guy said, "It is fucking dark out here."

Another asked, "Where is your weapon?"

I replied, "I don't have one."

He asked, "Are you nuts?"

"We could debate who it nuts," I said. "But I'll leave you in the jungle." We all laughed, and I asked if they knew my friend, Pete Fellini.

One of them said, "Yes. He is on his third tour."

I responded, "When you see him, tell him I said hi." Just then, we heard a plane fly by, and we saw a large ball of fire on a mountain. That light of fire hadn't been there before. I heard three clicks on my radio. I said, "Hang on," and headed to the beach.

One guy said, "I can't see shit. Are you sure we are going the right direction?"

I said, "Yes." As we got closer, I said, "Listen to the waves hitting the beach." All went quiet, and I landed my vessel on the beach. They all jumped off, waved, and started to blend into the jungle. I backed out and headed back. When I felt it was safe, I put my running lights on. I must say, it felt good when I finally saw the shore lights. I pulled my vessel up on land, reported to the OD, told him the mission was completed with no trouble, left, and went to bed.

The next morning, I left with my support team. When we reached base, we went our separate ways. I reported to Sarge and told him I was back. He replied, "Great. I will put you on tomorrow's roster."

I entered my tent and saw Dave sitting on his cot, looking very sad. I asked him what was bothering him. He looked up and said, "My ma said my wife is three months pregnant." I did not know what to say, and the next few weeks he was feeling down. One day, I wrote to my friend Maddy and asked if she would write him. She agreed, and after a few months, Dave's spirit was looking good.

CHAPTER 25

One day, I headed for my vessel with my partner, Lee (a White Rock marine from Korea), and Took; we had started patrols, as well as carrying cargo. I said, "Took, I'm leaving you on the barge anchored in the center of the bay to guard. Remember, fuck what the officer said. If you see someone or something coming toward you, shoot it."

The radio started to bark, saying, "249 lead toward the pontoon bridge."

I reminded the guys, "Remember what I said," before starting for the bridge. I was about halfway to the bridge when I heard gunfire coming from the barge. I turned and headed back to the barge, and we saw a boat speeding away. Lee opened fire, but they were too far away. I radioed to HQ, telling them what was happening. I moored to the barge and started looking for Took; I wasn't sure if he was in the water or on the barge. We found him lying on the barge floor. I bent down and looked at him. He had taken a shot to the head, but he was awake, saying, "I should have listened to you." Lee came up with a first aid kit. As he bandaged Took's head, I radioed HQ. They told us to stand by; they were sending out a boat with a medic.

They loaded Took on the vessel and left, while telling me to moor to the barge and guard it until they could figure out what to do with the barge. I turned all the lights out and waited, Lee and I did talk to each other for a while, then we went into our own thoughts. Eventually, we both heard the rowing of oars at the same time; Lee quietly untied my boat. In my mind I kept saying, "Shit, shit. Do I chase, stay, shoot, call?" I only had seconds to make my decision. I said to myself, "What the fuck. You can only die once." I whispered to Lee, "Safety off." He nodded his head, and I started the engines. As soon as I did, we heard the rowing increase. I put my spot light where I believed the boat would be.

We saw a girl, a boy, and an old man with a fishing net. They knew not to be on the water at night. Lee started speaking to them in Vietnamese, and I could see fish in the boat. The boy and girl looked scared; Lee looked at me like, "What now?"

I told him to yell at them and tell them that they would be shot next time they were caught on the water and that they needed to go home immediately. Lee smiled and told them. We watched them row toward shore, then I went back to the barge and waited, hoping I made the right decision. As the sun was coming up, I heard our replacement coming. When I got back to base, I pulled my sea plugs so the bilge's pumps could drain. Then, I went to my tent, where I found a letter from Judy on my cot.

(Don't let anyone tell you different. All soldiers love mail, and when they don't get any, they are very sad, especially around the holidays.) I held Judy's letter in my hand as I started to shake, thinking I could have just killed three innocent people. I had no problem killing if I had to, but I just wanted to be sure I was killing the enemy.

Dave walked in the tent, looked at me, and said, "Why the face?" I told him, and he said, "Pete, fuck the world. You must do whatever it takes to get home to Judy. Remember, the decision you make is the right decision at that time. Look I got a letter from Maddy, and I see you got a letter from Judy." Laughing, he continued, "Let's read them together."

I opened my letter. While reading it I exclaimed, "Shit." Dave asked what was wrong, so I replied, "Judy would like me to become Catholic, so we can be married on the other side of the gates like her sisters. But she said I don't have to if I don't want to."

Dave said, "What gates?"

I said, "Beats the shit out of me, but if she wants it, I'll do it. I know it will not sit well with my mom though."

Dave laughed and asked, "Why?"

I replied, "My mother is a WASP, which is a White Anglo-Saxon Protestant."

Dave shrugged his shoulders, saying, "You're marrying Judy, not your mother. Worry about it when the time comes."

"Good point," I replied.

CHAPTER 26

The next morning Dave and I checked the roster and saw that we were on the same shift. Sarge came out and said, "You two will take the two containers of beds up to General Westmore's officer barracks. It's a shame the wounded and sick have to sleep on cots when the officers get beds." Then, he went inside his office.

We loaded our vessels and headed for the officers' barracks. Dave was the lead; he looked back at me, and I gave him a thumbs-up. With my signal, we headed to the hospital. When we pulled up, we cut the seals ("seals" means it was inspected and sealed before leaving port) and told the orderly that the beds arrived and must be unloaded quickly. I had never seen so many people run out and to grab and move beds. There were nurses, doctors, and wounded; it was a group comprising whoever could perform physical labor. Once the containers were empty, the head nurse came out and thanked us, giving us each a kiss on the cheek while whispering in our ears, "Hope you don't get into too much trouble."

We took the empty containers back to the holding area and went back to base, finding Sarge there waiting for us. He said, "Come with me," so we went into his office. He proceeded to call the officer in charge of the barracks and said, "Sir, I have the men who took the beds to be delivered. They thought the beds were for the wounded and sick, so they delivered them to the hospital. If you want, I will send them back to get them." Smiling, he continued after listening to the officer's response, "Yes sir, I promise I will not allow them to deliver the next shipment. Yes sir, I promise I will reprimand them." He hung up the phone, and smiling he said, "OK you two, you're pulled off the front. You'll be going home soon, so you both will be water boys [driving the tankers to get water]. Dismissed."

Dave and I walked out laughing. I said, "You know, Dave, we spent a year in 'Nam and never fired a shot, and we are both expert rifle men."

Dave turned and said, "Don't jinx us."

After chow, I went to the Catholic church and met Father Casmir. I explained to him that I wanted to change to follow the Catholic denomination and why I wanted to convert. He said, "To change denominations just to go through the gates is not a good reason."

I then said, "If I change, we will have one house of the same religion."

He replied, "OK, that is better. You can start your religion instructions tomorrow." He then gave me a bunch of books to read.

I was doing well; it was December, and in a few more weeks I would be finished with my conversion to becoming a Catholic and would be going home. I was walking to my tent when Sarge called me over and said, "The Captain wants to see you. Try not to lose your temper."

I walked into his office, saluted him, and said, "You wanted to see me, sir."

He replied, "Yes. I'm sending you to Qui-Nhon; I need an experienced person."

"Sir, I was called off the front. I will be going home in two weeks. I must finish my religion instructions before I go home, and I'm taking a test tonight," I replied.

He said, "I will call Father Casmir now." After the phone connected he continued, "Father, this is Captain Peterson. Wolfinger will not be going to see you for a couple of days… Yes, I know his tour is over, but I need him…. No father, I will not send him. You're a priest, and I'm a captain…

Yes, Colonel Casmir, he will be there." He then turned to me and said, "You're dismissed."

I went to church that night, and as I sat down to take my test, I thanked the Father for helping me. Though I did tell him that I wasn't afraid to go, I also said that this was very important to me, and I knew there wasn't time for a second chance. He put his hand on my shoulder while saying, "I know you weren't afraid to go. You did your duty. Now, it's time to go home and marry the woman that is waiting for you. Let me ask you some questions." As he quizzed me with questions, I answered to the best of my ability. At the end, he said, "Good, you passed. Now I will baptize you into the Catholic church."

After he baptized me, he handed me the baptism paper and said, "Go in peace, my son."

CHAPTER 27

A few days later, Dave and I stood in our tent, dressed in our tropical uniforms. Looking around, we were lost in our own thoughts. Eventually, I said "Can you believe we spent 11 months and 29 days here?"

Dave smiled and said, "The best part is, we made it." We both went into our own thoughts again, but we were suddenly pulled out of them when we heard Sarge yell, "Let's go, or you'll be here another year."

We arrived at the airport, said our goodbyes, and headed for our gate. This time we were going home on an eastbound airline plane. A recruiter walked us to the plane, offering Dave and I rank and bonuses if we would stay six months longer. Dave started to weaken, but I said, "Not me. I'm going home, and I don't give a flying shit what they want to give me."

After a long time traveling, the final landing was in Washington state. The pilot was great; he flew one time in a circle and banked to each side, so we could see the Christmas lights. When we landed, there were heated buses waiting for us, and we were taken to a building where they took measurements for our Army greens. Then, we had lunch, which consisted of all you could eat and drink steak and milk. They had our suits finished and our orders cut by the time we finished lunch.

Before we knew it, we were put on a bus and headed back to the airport. We were walking through the terminal when a group of hippies started calling us "baby killers." We all stopped; there were about 20 of us. We put our bags down and started toward them, but the sergeant said, "Stop it. It is their right to speak freely. That is what we fought for, and if we hit them, then we fought for nothing." Then, a hippie came up to him and spat on him. In response, the sergeant hit the hippie so hard, he went over the chairs. The other hippies ran, and he put his hand up to stop us from chasing them. He then walked over to the knocked out hippie and took his bandanna from his head to wipe the spit off of his uniform. He walked back over to us and said, "Except when they touch us." We said our goodbyes and headed our separate ways.

Dave and I boarded a plane heading for New York (yep, Dave came home with me). The plane was empty, so they put us in first class. The steward-esses even gave us free drinks and flirted with us. They wanted us to go home with them when we landed; I told Dave, "You can go; I'm not."

We landed, and I took a cab to Judy's house first. I knocked on the door, and when she opened it, she screamed with joy while hugging and kissing me. I introduced Dave to Judy. We stayed a few minutes before I gently let go of Judy and said, "We have to go; we have a cab waiting, and I haven't been home yet."

We walked up the steps and entered my parents' apartment. They all jumped up and came running to me. My grandparents heard the noise, came in, and hugged me. When everything settled down, I introduced Dave to everyone. I looked at my father; his jet-black hair was gray. My mother noticed me looking at his hair as he was talking to Dave, and she quietly said, "Every time we got a letter from you the TV showed that place being attacked." That was the first time I realized our war was a TV war. My sister and my brother-in-law, Jerry, said, "Please stay at our house while you are on leave. We have a guest room with two beds." Before I could say anything, Dave accepted their offer.

My brother Charlie gave me the keys to his car and said, "Use it as long as you're home. My girlfriend, Connie, has a car."

I thanked him while taking the keys and said, "I'll keep her full." We both laughed.

Dave asked to use the phone to call Maddy, and Maddy said she would meet him at my sister's house, so we said our so longs and headed for my sister's house.

My sister and Jerry showed us the room and said, "Make yourselves at home."

We thanked them while telling them, "Please, do not touch us to wake us up or come up behind us." My sister looked sad, and Jerry looked nervous.

That night Judy and I sat in the car, hugging and talking. She said, "Let's get married as soon as possible. I agreed, so we decided to go home and tell our families.

We went to Judy's parents. They were upset, saying we should wait until I got out of the Army. Judy said, "No. We are getting married as soon as we can."

Judy's father said, "I hope you are not considering getting married by the justice of the peace."

Judy replied, "No, I'll have a wedding like you want, but it will happen as soon as we can have it."

He walked away, saying, "I give you six months."

Judy's mother said, "OK, but I agree with your father, it won't last."

We left and headed for my parents' house. When we told my parents, we got the same response. They said, "It won't last. You both should wait." When we said refused, they said, "We wish you the best."

Once in the car, Judy said, "We have a lot to do. Let's look for a hall first, then a church. The rest I can do while you are away. You can meet me after work, and we can start looking."

I looked surprised and said, "You've been going to work while I'm home?"

She smiled while putting my face between her hands kissing me and said, "Yes, we will need the money."

CHAPTER 28

Dave and I were having some trouble adjusting to being home. When on a double date, a car backfired, and we both hit the ground. Everyone just looked at us, but we just got up and laughed. The girls thought we were nuts. When sleeping, we would wake up at any sound we heard and quietly go through the house, making sure not to wake up my sister and Jerry.

One day I came back to my sister's house early; she called me to the kitchen. I went to the kitchen, and I saw her crying, and our knives were laid out on the kitchen table. She looked at me and said, "I found these when changing the sheets. Why? And why are you and Dave roaming the house at night? You scare us. We don't open the door when we hear you. What have they done to you?"

I hugged her and said, "Sis, it is hard to explain, but if you want us to leave, I understand. We can get a hotel."

Through her tears she said, "Never."

After she calmed down, we talked about my wedding, and when I felt she was OK, I took the knives and went to my bedroom. I put the knifes back under the pillow and changed.

The weeks went fast, and before I knew it, our leave was up. Judy and I found a hall and church. The wedding date was set for March 9. We said our goodbyes and headed back to Fort Story, Virginia.

We were assigned to a barrack with other returning veterans. We automatically bonded and became brothers with the men in our barracks. After settling in, I went to headquarters and asked Private Jones to speak to the sergeant in charge. I entered the sergeant's office and said, "I request to put in leave to get married," and handed him the papers.

He looked up and said, "I will review it and let you know."

I was shocked and said, "But Sarge, I'm getting married."

He looked up and said, "One, my name is Sergeant White, and you will address me as such. Second, I told you that I would let you know. Now please, leave my office."

I left and went right to the church where I asked to see the priest, who was not there. I went back to the barracks cursing. The next morning, we had 0800 formation. We stood at ease as Sergeant White called out our names; then, he called us to attention, and Lieutenant Wills stepped forward and said, "At ease. While I understand most of you are waiting to be discharged, you are still a solider in the United States Army and will act like one. You will salute officers and wait for their return salute. You will address you fellow soldiers by their correct rank and name, and you will have shined boots and clean uniforms. There will be a roster posted every day, naming the people who have details to do. Weekends are free unless you are on detail. The commander will have an open door policy every other night from 6 to 9."

I spoke to the Captain during open door policy, and he assured me that my leave would be signed and Dave's also. The captain was also overseas, and he knew what we were all going through. He asked us to have patience. He was well aware of what every returning soldier was going through, being one himself.

The next day Sergeant White gave Dave and me our leave papers along with KP (kitchen duty) for the weekend.

CHAPTER 29

The day of my wedding, I stood in front of the church door, waiting for the church to open. I was nervous and couldn't sleep the night before or stand still. I could not believe the day had finally come. When the doors opened, I went to the altar and waited, deep in my own thoughts. The rest of the wedding party came in with the guests. Judy was late, and I started to think that she had changed her mind or that my sister had told her about my knife under the pillow. When she appeared in the doorway, she looked beautiful. As we said our vows (past the open white gates), the priest smiled at Judy and said, "Please, don't be late next time, and please, help Pete with the ring before he takes your finger off." He finished our vows, and we kissed and left the church for pictures and the reception. It was a great day for all.

We left the wedding hall and headed for our hotel room. Once in the hotel room, we started to relax. I helped her unbutton her wedding dress, then she went into the bathroom. When she stepped out, she was totally naked, except for a sheer white negligee and white high heels. She looked like she stepped out of a Playboy magazine. She slowly walked toward me, giving me a chance to take in all her beauty. When she got close, she looked up at me; now that I could see her face, which I really wasn't paying much attention to, I could see she was blushing. I kissed her while picking her up and laying her on the bed. I started very slowing caressing her body, assuring her I would stop anything she wanted, which she didn't. We made passionate love throughout the night. The next day, we left her wedding dress at the front desk for her father to pick up, and headed for our plane to Puerto Rico. Once in our room we made love, took a shower, and headed for the beach.

Judy laid on the sand, sunning herself as I was swimming. After about 30 minutes, I came ashore and suggested to Judy that we go up because we were in a tropical sun and you could get burnt really fast. She replied, "Not to worry. I always get a good tan by staying in the sun longer."

I did not want to argue on our honeymoon, so I said, "Be careful," and headed up to our room. About a ½ hour later, Judy came in, looking like a red lobster. She took a shower and came out, saying she was chilly and did not feel well, I helped her into bed; then, I called for the hotel doctor. He came and inspected Judy. He told me she had sun poisoning and she needed to be kept in bed and given hot tea. He also informed me that blisters would form, and we should not break them. "They will break on their own, and it will hurt," he informed us. "In about four days, she will feel better."

I slept on the couch for four days. She would cry and tell me how sorry she was and that she would make it up to me. I would just smile and tell her not to worry and that she just needed to get well. By the fifth day, she felt great and had a beautiful tan. To celebrate, we went to the casino next door, had dinner, and played roulette. The following day, we headed for home. We went to her parents' home first, then mine. That night we stayed in a hotel, and the next morning we just stayed in the hotel until it was time for me to get ready to fly back that evening. We went back to Judy's parents' apartment. I left Charlie's car with her, called for a cab, and headed for the airport.

CHAPTER 30

I was unpacking my bag when Dave came in smiling, saying that it was good to see me. I replied, saying "Staying out of trouble?"

He said, "Sure am. I got my divorce, so now I can marry Maddy."

Sergeant Shithead did a surprise inspection, taking everything that was not authorized. Man, I have never seen so many different types of weapons. The guys were really pissed off. Sergeant Shithead and Lieutenant Poop Brains were breaking balls any way they could. I said "Dave, let's just stay by the sidelines and watch. I would like to go home when we can, and we still have three months left."

I would call Judy every night for about 10 minutes. One night, she told me that she took the car to get gas and a police car pulled next to her, asking her to pull over. She didn't. She drove off, parked the car, and ran up to her apartment. The police officers came to the front door, saw my mother-in-law smoking out the window, and asked if she has seen a pretty blonde. She replied, "Yes, she is up here." The officer asked if they could come up, and she said, "Sure."

Once in the kitchen, the officer asked Judy, "Why didn't you stop? I wanted to ask you out."

Judy replied, "I'm married, and I was scared."

He asked, "May I see your license?"

Judy said, "I don't have one." So, he gave her a ticket and left.

As she was telling me the story, I was telling her, "Don't worry. Take the money we have saved, and go to court."

Crying she said, "My father said he won't go with me because I shouldn't have been driving."

I said, "Judy, I can't get home for two weeks. Sarge is on the war path and canceled all leaves. Call Charlie."

She said, "No, I will go myself. I love you."

I replied, saying, "I love you, too, but why didn't you wait until I got home?"

She replied, "I miss you and want to spend as much time together as we can. By the time you get home and find a hotel, there is hardly any time for us to be together." Then, she started crying.

I said, "Don't cry. It won't be much longer. I love you. I'll talk to you to-morrow night."

After I got off the phone I told Dave. He said, "Now that is true love."

Judy stood before the judge in night court, by herself, not knowing her father was in the back of the courtroom. The judge said, "How do you plead?"

Judy replied, "Guilty, your honor," in shaky voice.

The judge asked, "Why were you driving without a license?"

Judy replied, "I was just married, and my husband just came home from overseas. He was going to be coming home on a two-day pass, and I wanted to have gas in the car for him."

The judge smiled and said, "OK, I will give you a wedding gift. You will only pay a $10 fine and promise not to drive until you have a driver's license."

When she left the courtroom, she saw her father standing there. She smiled and said, "Dad you came."

He replied, "I wanted to teach you a lesson, so I sat in the back, in case you needed money, but you did good. Now let's go home."

I called that night (I always called late because the rates were cheaper). I listened to her tell me about her adventure with court. Since our house was rented out, we had to find an apartment. Judy's cousin Aggie found a one-bedroom apartment close to her job. She wanted to know if she should get it before someone else did. She said when I got up there we could start looking for furniture. I said, "Sure, why not?"

CHAPTER 31

It was almost the end of April when Dave and I flew up to New York for the weekend. We left on a Friday night and would return on Sunday night. Maddy picked us up and dropped me off at Judy's parents' apartment. Judy was waiting for me in the car. I got in, and we headed for a motel. (My parents' apartment was too small, and Judy parents felt uncomfortable with me sleeping in Judy's bedroom, which was next to theirs.)

The next day Judy showed me the apartment and what Aggie and her were doing to it, so it would be ready when I came home. Then we went looking for furniture. Man I never knew there were so many types of furniture, and I do believe we looked at them all, but we were happy. That evening as we sat at the dinner, Judy talked about how nice it was going to be once I was out of the Army. I reminded her that I didn't have a job, but I did pass the police exam before I was drafted. Judy's whole face changed, from mad to sad to crying so hard that people were looking at me like I did something to her. I left money on the table, stood up, and asked Judy if we could finish the discussion in the car before I got into a fight with someone. She shook her head yes. As she got up, I put my arm around her and started walking to the door. I could feel the eyes and hear the whispers as we walked to the door.

Once in the car, I asked, "Why are you crying?"

She hugged me tight, put her head into my chest, and started sobbing. I could barely make out the words, "I don't want to lose you."

I gently pushed her away from me, which was difficult as I hadn't realized how strong she was, and said, "What the hell are you talking about?"

Between sobs, she told me that she didn't want me to become a police officer because she could have lost me once and didn't want to chance losing me again. I said, "OK, I won't join. Is that it?"

She shook her head no and hugged me again. I said, "Judy, you have to talk to me, so I know what I'm doing wrong."

She leaned back, and I handed her a few napkins that I had in my pocket. She started crying again. I said, "Please, Judy, please try not to cry. Just tell me what is bothering you."

All of a sudden she said, "I know you sleep with a knife under your pillow, and it scares me. And sometimes, you have a blank look on your face, and that scares me. And I know there is something that happened to you, and I know you won't tell me." Then, she started crying while saying, "I love you," and started hugging me.

I said, "Judy, I can't tell you why I put the knife under the pillow, but I promise I will not do it again. I will give the knife to Dave tomorrow. I will leave it in the trunk for tonight. And the stares, I go into deep thought about how am I going to provide for you."

She grabbed me and started kissing me, saying, "Let's go to the motel. I have to fix my make-up and do a few other things."

That night she fell asleep in my arms as I lay awake looking at the ceiling. Morning came; Judy woke up, still in my arms, looked at me, and gave me a long loving kiss, which led to passionate lovemaking. Then, she got up and took a shower. When she got out, it was my turn. I needed that shower to wake me up before we headed to breakfast. We spent the day looking at more furniture, to make sure we had chosen the right furniture. That night Maddy met us at Judy's parents' apartment, and we all went out for dinner; then, the girls dropped us off at the airport.

I didn't get back home for May because I was getting ready to get out in June and we were trying to save as much money as we could. Sergeant White made sure we were busy. The weekends were the hardest part; Dave wouldn't go back to New York without me, so, we would exchange our free time for a price to those who had KP or some other task assigned to them on the weekends. Thankfully, Sergeant White didn't seem to care as long as the task got done, which really surprised a lot of us.

CHAPTER 32

June 19 finally came, and Sergeant White gave Dave and I our discharge papers and told us, "Thank you for your service." Despite his kind words, his face seemed to say, "Now get the hell out of my office."

When we arrived at the airport in New York, Maddy was waiting for us. I asked where Judy was, and she said, "She is waiting at your new apartment."

When we got to the building, I asked if they were coming up, but Maddy and Dave declined, saying they would come over another time. Then, they smiled and took off. I walked up the steps and opened the door. Everyone yelled, "Welcome home!" Both our families were there, and I was surprised that everyone fit in the apartment. We had a great time that day, and at the end of the evening I thanked everyone for coming. After everyone left, Judy smiled and said to me, "Now for the real dessert."

The next day, Dave and Maddy came up to see our apartment. We were sitting at the kitchen table when Dave said, "I have to tell you something, and I feel bad telling you."

I said, "Spit it out."

Dave said, "You and Judy can't come to our wedding." Before I could ask why, he continued, "Maddy's father said you betrayed him by introducing me, a divorced man, to his only daughter, and if you come, he will not pay for the wedding. Pete, I don't have the money to pay for it."

I replied, "Don't worry. I know how Catholics are, not allowing divorced persons to marry in a Catholic church; my cousin went through it. Where are you getting married?"

Dave said, "We found a protestant church that Maddy's father approves of."

I said, "Great, we'll celebrate later."

I had to start looking for a job, which was not easy. The war I was in did not help me. While I was job hunting, I met some other veterans who told me to not say I'm a veteran; if I followed that advice, they said I may get a job. I politely replied, "Fuck them." During this time, a lot of veterans were turning to drugs, drinking, or living in the woods. I'm not sure how we knew we were brothers in arms, but when we would see another veteran, we would just smile and say, "Welcome home" (which still happens today).

I had some problems myself, which started to show up. I started sleeping out of the bed and in the corner of the bedroom where I could see the entrance of the door to our bedroom.

Dave and I would meet at the diner on Atlantic Avenue for coffee before we would go job hunting. We would bring each other up-to-date on what was happening. Dave said that he and Maddy had found an apartment around the corner from Maddy's parents and that she was pregnant. I just smiled. He said, "What? She got pregnant on our honeymoon."

"Sure she did," I responded. Then we both laughed. I told Dave of my problem and asked if he was having the same. He said he wasn't, and he couldn't believe I would leave a bed with a beautiful woman like Judy still in it for any reason. I said, "Dave, this is no joke. Judy is getting scared."

He replied, "Still keep your knife under the pillow?" When I said I didn't, he said, "There is your problem. Remember after John, we were all on edge even with our knifes; then we got Drip Drop." (Drip Drop was a dog we saved and brought back to base after we watched her being beaten to death so she could be eaten by some local women. We named her Drip Drop because Dave had the clap at the time. We kept her in our tent, and she would bark as soon as anyone would enter the tent, which made us feel safe.) Dave continued, "There is your solution, a dog. Let's get you a dog."

I said, "I don't know."

He asked, "You want to stay in bed with Judy?" So we paid for the coffee and went dog hunting. We ended up at Pine Kennels and bought a shepherd that was already house trained and listened to basic commands. On the way home I told Dave, "I'm glad Judy got rid of the knife. If she doesn't

like this, she might use it on me." We got to the apartment and went upstairs to wait for Judy. As soon as Judy saw the dog, she fell in love with her. Without asking, she turned to me and said, "Let's call her Silver."

Upon hearing that, Dave said, "My job is done, brother. See you tomorrow." Then, he left.

CHAPTER 33

The next day at the diner, Dave and I talked about the dog and Maddy. When we finished our coffee, I said, "Let's go to the big companies in Manhattan."

Dave said, "No, I stand a better chance checking the car dealers that need a mechanic." We left and went our separate ways, not knowing if we would see each other for a while.

I went to Manhattan and started job searching; a lot of companies took my name and said they would call me. (Dave said a lot of the guys with jobs were draft dodgers.) My last stop before heading home was the utility company; the interviewer asked me where I last worked, and I told him the Army. He replied, "Hell, I was in the Korea war. Welcome home, brother." Then he shook my hand while saying, "I have a job for you. The department is called the I&A (installation and apparatus). Its nickname is the insane asylum; it is dangerous work, but it pays good money. And there is a lot of overtime."

I looked at him and said, "Where do I sign?"

"Go upstairs to room 1210 and ask for O'Hara. I'll call ahead."

I thanked him and left. As I sat down, Mr. O'Hara said. "I'm told you're a veteran."

I said to myself, "Here it comes, no job." I replied, "Yes."

He said, "Great. I was in World War 2. Where you're going most are vets. Now for your test." He laid a ruler on the desk and asked what it was.

I replied, "A ruler."

"Good. Now what is this?" he continued as he laid down a wrench.

I replied, "An adjustable wrench."

He said, "Great. Go to room 1245 for the doctor to see you. When you are done, come back."

While the doctor was examining me, he noticed my foot and asked what happened. I told him a shell hit it while in 'Nam, and I did not say anything about it until I got state side. The Army doctor wanted to take the toe off, which meant learning how to walk again and staying in the Army six months longer. I told him no. He smiled and said, "Can you wear work boots?"

I said, "Yes, I'm wearing them now," and pointed to my Army boots.

He said, "Great, you're approved. Go see O'Hare."

I said, "Thank you," and went to see O'Hare.

O'Hare said, "Everything looks good. Go to the 20th floor, show the photo guy this paper, and he will take a picture and give you an ID card. Then, report to flushing yard and see a Mr. Keane on Monday."

By the time I got home, Judy was cooking dinner. I hugged her and said, "I got a job with the electric company."

She hugged me back and asked, "Is it dangerous?"

I said "No," while kissing her. I continued, "I've got to call Dave."

Dave answered the phone, and I told him that I had gotten a job with the electric company. Dave replied, "I got one too, with Chrysler as a diesel mechanic, starting Monday."

Judy said, "Ask them over for dinner. We have enough, and we can celebrate."

Dave heard her and said, "Great, I'll bring the beer."

That night we sat around the table, laughing and joking. Dave said, "How is Silver working out?"

I said, "She is great."

He sadly said, "I miss Drip Drop."

I told him, "She is being spoiled by the new guys."

He smiled and said, "You're probably right." The night went fast, and before we knew it, it is was midnight. We decided we had better call it a night because the next day was Sunday, and we had to rest up for our new jobs.

CHAPTER 34

I met Mr. Keane at his office. He laid down the rules, which included that workers were not allowed to be out for 90 days (if you were, you were fired—no excuses) and after 90 days you were required to join the union. Then, he gave me an address to report to. He said, "It is a vault project, and Frank and John will give you OJT (on the job training)."

I thanked him and headed for the job location. I arrived to see two men sitting on what looked like a large tool cart having coffee. I walked over and introduced myself, and they did the same. John had seven kids and was in the Navy. Frank was single and was in the Army, but he was now in the Army reserves. After our introductions, Frank said the following, "Always show up for work. When connecting cable, remember neutral on first when connecting, neutral off last when removing." Then he showed me a set of test lamps. "These are your lifeline; always test both ends of the cable before connecting. If they light up, don't connect them. We will teach you more later."

The day went fast, and I really felt at ease. I reported to that location at 8 a.m. every day. Frank would call the office and give them updates. Once in a while, Mr. Keane would come by and check on the job. My job was to lay out the cable and pump the foot press for them when they were making a connection. Man, the cable was heavy, and my legs got tired real fast pumping the foot press. I could see why these guys had big arms. I looked like an undernourished kid next to them.

The time was flying by. I was in my second month of probation when I received a letter from the VA saying I must report to them one week from that day. I get the letter to the foreman, Sam. He came back the next day and said I couldn't go, and if I did go, I would be fired. Sam said, "It's not my call; the decision came from the general foreman, Mr. Pots."

I asked Frank who Mr. Pots was, and Frank replied, "He's a miserable person, who would fuck you any chance he can. Don't fuck with him." At lunch time I went to the phone and called the VA; a lady answered, and I explained the problem. I told her I would not be able to go. The lady got really mad and asked for Mr. Pots' name and location. I gave her the information as she requested while saying, "Please, I don't want trouble."

She replied, "Young man, do not worry, you won't," and hung up.

The next day a black sedan pulled up to our location, and a tall man got out and stood by the car. Frank saw him and said, "That is Pots. You're fucked."

Mr. Pots asked me to come to him, and as I stood before him, I was thinking, "What am I going to tell Judy when he fires me?" The car window came down just a little, and cigar smoke came out. The person in the car said, "Tell him."

All eyes were on him as he spoke; he said, "I'm sorry for denying you to go to the VA. You can go and will not be fired." The voice from the window continued, "And Pots said you will be paid for the day and any overtime you may miss."

I said, "Thank you," but he did not respond. He just got in the car and left. Frank, laughing, said, "I don't care who you are, don't fuck with the government. Now let's get back to work."

The next week, I sat on the doctor's examination table at the VA hospital. He looked at my left foot and asked, "Who cut the side and removed the nail?"

I said, "A doctor in the VA hospital in Virginia."

He then asked, "Feel any pain?"

I said, "Sometimes."

He said, "OK, put your boots on, and you can leave."

It was late October. I had finished my probation and become a member of the local 1-2 utility union. To celebrate, Frank and John bought me breakfast at the diner. I noticed that John and Frank were growing beards, so I asked, "What's with the beards?"

John said, "Winter is coming, and a lot of blood money overtime will start from burnouts. That means climbing poles and staying on top of the service boxes and manholes. When the wind hits your face, you will be glad you had a beard."

CHAPTER 35

The year was 1968, and winter was here, and I did grow my beard. Like the men said, the ladies were not happy. The first storm hit, and it hit hard. Frank said to me, "Let's see how you did on your training. Climb that pole and fix that hanging leg." (The average utility pole is 44 feet high, and when you are that high, the pole sways a little. The hardest part is leaning back and trusting your belt will hold you. By doing this, your hands are free to work.)

I said, "OK."

Frank watched as I climbed the pole; the wind was strong, and snow was hitting my face. I could still hear Frank yelling, "Move it! It's cold out here." When I reached the top, I wrapped my arms around the pole and hung onto it, like you would your wife. I was nervous to let go. I did it a lot in training, but now it felt different. I heard Frank yell, "Stop making love to the pole and fix the leg. If you fall, I will catch you." That brought a smile to my face, and I finally let go, trusting my belt.

I fixed the leg and came down to see Frank laughing. I said, "Hey, that was my first time."

Frank said, "I know, kid. You did good. I'm laughing because your beard is full of ice. Let's sit in the truck and warm up."

The winter was a long hard brutal winter. Judy was getting upset because she hardly saw me, so I promised her when spring came, we would go anywhere is wanted. Spring did come, but it took its time.

CHAPTER 36

It was July 1969, and I had one year in the company, giving me two weeks' vacation. While having coffee, I was telling Frank and John where I would like to take Judy for vacation. Just then, Karl the foreman pulled up with a truck behind him. He got out of his car and walked over to us. As he was walking over to us, a very large man was getting out of the truck. Once we were all together, Karl introduced me to Big Bill and told us they were short on helpers, so I would be working with Big Bill. We spoke for a little while longer; then Karl said, "Better go, Bill. You got an appointment." We said our so longs and started for the truck.

While driving to the location, Bill, who stood 6'6" and weighed about 340 pounds, told me that he never was in the service. He got married young and had eight kids: six boys, two girls. I then told him about myself. Before you knew it, we had arrived at our location.

Bill said, "See if anyone is home while I get the tools."

I got out of the truck and knocked on the customer's door, and a little old Italian lady answered. She couldn't have been more than 5'2", and she looked up at me, standing 6'2", while saying, "Mamma mia, you're big." And then she looked at Bill and said, "You two are going to break my house." I assured her we wouldn't, and she let us in. We headed for the basement, and as we walked down the basement stairs, Bill, who was on the third step, went through the step. The lady screamed, "You're breaking my house. Get out!"

Bill said to the lady, "You're lucky I didn't break my leg." We climbed back up the steps, and once we both got on the platform, the old lady started hitting us with a broom while yelling. She kept saying that we were breaking her house and chased us out of the house with the broom. When we got outside, she locked the door and said we couldn't come back in. We called the office told them what happened.

Karl showed up with a small Italian guy named Rudy; they went and spoke to the lady. Karl, who was also 6'2," was not allowed in, but she did let Rudy in. After a few minutes, Rudy came out and said he could fix the step and do the electrical connection. Karl said, "OK, put the wood on your expense account." He then walked over to us, calling us "house wreckers" and said, "Go do street lights on Northern Boulevard."

Bill and I laughed the rest of the day. That night at dinner I told Judy about it; she just smiled and said, "Your father called. The tenants moved out."

I called my father, and he said we should meet him at the lawyer's office Saturday morning at about 10 a.m.

I said we would be there and then told Judy; she did not seem happy. That Saturday we all signed the required papers, and my father gave us the keys and said the mortgage is up-to-date. Judy and I went over and checked the house out; it needed work. The railing almost came off in Judy's hand. The kitchen only had a stove, nothing else. Upstairs was an old-fashioned bathroom, and it had no electric lights in the middle room.

The following week, Dave helped me move, and after we finished moving, Dave said quietly, "Our tent in 'Nam was better than this."

That Monday we went to work, and when we came home, we would try to do something to the house. Judy was getting quiet and not eating; then one day, she didn't get out of bed. I asked her what was wrong, but she said it was nothing. She just didn't feel well. I called the doctor, and he came to the house and went into our bedroom to examine Judy. He told me to stay outside. After about 20 minutes, he came out. I said, "Well?"

He looked in my face and said, "She is depressed, and by keeping it inside, it is making her sick."

I asked, "Depressed about what?"

He said, "Look around. You call this living?"

I said, "She never said nothing to me."

He replied, "Because she loves you and does not want to hurt your feelings. You better do something, or you will lose her, and I don't mean to another man. I gave her a sedative." Then he picked up his bag and left. I checked and saw that she was sleeping. I went around the corner to see my father and ask if he could help. As usual, he was in the shop. I explained everything to him; he listened, then put his hat on and said, "Let's go." The next thing I knew, we were sitting in Richmond Hill Savings Bank. He said, "My son would like a home improvement loan, and I will cosign for him."

We left the bank, and I thanked and hugged father. I went into our bedroom, and Judy was just waking up. I said, "Judy, we have money to fix the house any way you want." I went on to explain everything. The next day, she got up and went to work like nothing had happened. With friends and family, we turned the run-down house into a doll house; anyone walking by would stop and admire the house and garden.

One day while sitting in the truck with Bill waiting for the next job to come in, I told Bill that the owner of the Van Wick Diner baked Judy a cake and asked her out. She told him she was married. Bill said, "We can't have that."

I said, "I told Judy I wouldn't start trouble. She gets her coffee there every day."

Bill said, "OK, let's just get coffee there and thank him for the cake."

We pulled up in front of the diner and walked over to the takeout counter. I asked for the owner, and eventually, the owner came over. I was sizing him up; he was 5' 8", nice looking, and of average build. He looked like a player, with a gold chain hanging around his neck. When he got to us, he looked up and said, "Can I help you?"

I replied, "We were in the neighborhood and stopped to get coffee, so I figured I should thank you for making my wife, Judy, a cake." His face went white.

He said, "No problem. She and her girlfriends are good customers, and I like to do something nice for them."

I said, "Great, how much for the coffee?" I paid, and we left. Bill and I laughed the rest of the day.

That night at dinner Judy asked if I had stopped by the diner. I said, "We were in the neighborhood, so we stopped and got coffee. And I thanked him for the cake, why?"

She said, "Oh, no reason. By the way, I was thinking of changing jobs. I have an interview this Wednesday evening. The owner said he would wait for me after work to interview me. Would you drive me?"

I said, "Sure, any reason you don't want the job you have now?"

She said, "No."

Wednesday came, and I drove her to the interview. She got out of the car and went in; she wasn't in more than 5 minutes when she came running out crying. She got into the car and said, "Let's go."

I asked, "What happened?"

She said, "Pete, please go. I don't want any trouble."

I asked again in a firm voice, "What happened?"

She started crying while saying, "He said I could have the job if I sat on his face after work."

"What?!"

She continued to say, "He said he fired the last girl because she said no."

I was out of the car before she could grab me. I heard her hollering as I went through the doors and into his office. He looked up, surprised, and said, "What do you want?" He had the snobbiest attitude. I didn't say a word; I walked up to his desk and grabbed his hair, thinking I would bang his head into the desk and leave. Instead, I had a wig in my hand. His eyes went wide, and he started to pull his chair back, but I was able to grab his head and bang it on the desk, breaking his nose. Blood was everywhere. He lifted his head like he couldn't believe what had just happened. I turned and walked out, climbing into the car.

On the way home, she turned to me and said, "You didn't do anything bad did you?"

I said, "No, and why do you want another job anyway?"

In-between the sobbing, she said, "Well, I'm not pregnant yet, and I'm 24, so I figured I would become a professional boss's secretary, like my sister Dotty."

I said, "Judy, we haven't been trying that long. Remember, Dr. Fishman said we should just relax with a bottle of wine and enjoy it, not make it a project."

She started crying again, hugging my arm and saying OK.

When we got home, we went upstairs and started to undress. She looked at my work clothes and said, "What are those red stains."

Without missing a beat, I said, "Ketchup splatted on me when I tried using it today at lunch." That night we just lay in bed, hugging each other and talking about everything and anything until we fell asleep.

CHAPTER 37

I t was May 1971. Bill and I sat in our truck waiting for a job to come over the radio. While talking, I told Bill about us trying to have a baby. He laughed, saying, "All women are different. Some you just look at them, like my Ann, and they get pregnant, and some you have to try a little harder. Tomorrow go to sick call and tell the doctor about your problem. He'll tell you what you have to do." (We had doctors on our main work locations.)

I went to medical the next day. The doctor gave me an address and told me to make an appointment with a doctor who was a specialist in this area.

I got into the truck and brought Bill up to date. He said, "Great, let's go now."

I asked, "Now, in a company truck?"

He looked at me and said, "Yep, this is important."

I said, "What about work?"

He replied, "I'm good at making up excuses if I have to."

I entered the doctor's office and gave the secretary the recommendation. I told her that this was the only time I could get there. She said, "Please sit down, and I will see if the doctor can see you." She came out and said, "Follow me," while bringing me into a room with a long metal examining table. She handed me a gown and left; then, the doctor came in, introduced himself, and instructed me to lay on the table face down and hold the edge of the examining table. He then told me, "This is going to feel uncomfortable, but it will be over quickly." The next thing I knew, I felt something long going up my ass. I almost flew off the table. He said, "I will give you the result in 15 minutes." Then he handed me napkins to wipe my ass and instructed me to wait outside once I got cleaned up.

Finally, the doctor came out, said that I could make babies like a rabbit, smiled, and left. I said to the secretary, "How much do I owe?"

She said, "Nothing, you are covered."

As I walked back to the truck, I could see Bill laughing. When I got into the truck, I asked, "What are you laughing about?"

Bill said, "You are walking like you had something shoved up your ass."

I replied, "I did, and now that I'm sitting down I feel like I shit my pants."

Bill started laughing so hard that I started laughing with him. We drove back to the yard as everyone was just leaving. Bill drove me to my car, so the guys couldn't see the back of my pants.

When I got home, I was just about to open the door, but Judy opened the door, grabbed me, and started hugging me and kissing me. As we stood there, she told me she was pregnant. I just smiled. She stepped back and asked, "What is wrong?" I then explained to her what I did and turned around to show her the back of my pants; she laughed so hard, she had to run to the bathroom. That night Judy, Silver, and I just sat on the couch, watching the fire going while listening to music. When we went to bed, I thanked the lord for all my blessings.

CHAPTER 38

It was the beginning of September, and the heat spell showed no signs of breaking, causing an overload on our system. We were working around the clock trying to keep it together. Bill and I were sitting in the truck, taking a break, when the office called telling us to head off to Continental Avenue in Kew Gardens. We were to meet Karl and the other crews. When we arrived, all the crews were working, and Karl was barking out orders; he turned and said, "You two, go to the SW service box and start connecting the sets of 500 that the cable gang just pulled in."

We pulled to the service box, set up our truck, and pulled the cover; the hole was too small for Bill, so I jumped in and started connecting the cable. Everyone was working as hard as they could, but the temporary cables were burning up as fast as they were being laid out on the streets. The other crews were trying to make temporary connections in other service boxes but couldn't get the connections to hold. I was on my last connection when I heard Bill yell, "Get out. Nothing's holding." I put the connection back on the rack and watched the rubber melt in front of my eyes. The explosion blew me back against the wall, then I felt hands pulling me up and water being splashed on me. My ears were ringing, and I couldn't open my eyes. I started to hear voices as someone placed a cold rag across my eyes. I heard Karl say, "Bill, help me get him into the car, and I will take him to the emergency room."

When we got to the hospital, they put me on a table and brought me right in. A doctor said, "I'm an eye doctor, and I'm going to give you a light sedative, so I can look at your eyes." The next thing I knew, I tried to open my eyes, but I could only see darkness. I heard the doctor telling me, "I believe I got all the copper out, but your eyes are sore. Keep the patches on for three days, then come see me."

I heard Karl say, "OK."

They helped me off the table, and as Karl was walking me to the car, he said, "I'll take you home."

I said, "What about Judy? She is pregnant. If she sees me like this, she could have the baby."

Karl got on the radio and reached out to Joe Romano. He said, "Joe, you're a volunteer fireman right?" Joe replied that he was, so Karl said, "Good, go over to Wolfie's house. Tell Judy, Pete had a small accident, but he is OK. Then stay there and be ready just in case." Joe agreed to the plan.

As Karl helped me out of the car, I heard Judy screaming, "Oh My God! What happened?"

Then I heard Joe say, "I can deliver babies if you need me." Once inside, Karl tried to explain to Judy, but she was crying, and yelling.

In the background, Joe kept saying, "I can deliver the baby if you need me." Karl told Joe wait outside, then he sat me down and helped Judy to calm down. Once she calmed down, Karl said, "Please call me if you need anything, and Pete, I will see you at 8 a.m. here in three days." Then he left. I could hear Judy sobbing, but I just sat quiet.

After a few minutes she said, "Let's go upstairs. You need a bath and to change your clothes." As Judy helped me out of my clothes and helped me get ready for the bath, she said, "What are these red marks on your chest?"

I said, "Probably sparks."

She started hitting me and crying while saying, "You promised me the job wasn't dangerous." I just stood there, then she said, "You're quitting."

I felt around until l I could get her into my arms, kissing her where I could and said, "No."

She pulled away and said, "Yes." I felt my way into the tub, and I said, "Let's talk about this when I get the patches off my eyes." The next three days were nothing but fighting, hugging, and fighting.

As Karl and I sat in the doctor's examination room, the doctor said, "I took the patches off. Now, open your eyes slowly and tell me what you see." I opened my eyes and saw the doctor with Karl in the background; I told him what I saw. He then examined my eyes, and he said, "I see no copper. You missed the bullet on this one, young man."

Karl dropped me off at our house and said, "I'll see you tomorrow."

As I entered the house, I saw Judy folding the wash. When she saw me, she jumped up and ran to me, kissing me and telling me how much she loved me. I asked if she was mad at me, and she said, "I'm mad, but I love you more. Just promise the first chance you get you will transfer out to an office job." I told her I would.

CHAPTER 39

It was late November, and my mother was over complaining that men are pigs. She and Judy and had gone for a walk on the avenue, and the workmen kept whistling and staring at Judy. "I kept yelling that she is pregnant," my mother explained. "And that still didn't stop them."

I let her holler about men, and when she was done, I said, "Mom, I am sure you told them off. [What I wanted to say was, "Mom any man in their right mind would look at a beautiful woman with a size 48 breasts. But what they don't know and see is when she takes the bra off, how the bra straps cut into her tender skin and how I put salve on the cuts to ease the pain or how her back hurts carrying those breasts. They are beautiful to look at, but they come with a cost."] Is there something I could do for you, Mom?"

She replied, "I came over to spend time with Judy and see if you are having a birthday party tomorrow."

I said, "No Mom, it is a Tuesday. We will have it on Saturday."

That night when going to bed, Judy said, "What do you want for your birthday?"

I said, "How about a baby boy?"

She said, "I'll try."

It was about 3 a.m. when I rolled over into something wet. I jumped up to see Judy getting dressed and putting a towel between her legs while talking to her mother. I got out of my wet clothes and put on some fresh ones. She was still talking to her mother when I said, "We have to go."

She said, "See you at the hospital mom," hung up, and asked, "Do you have the suitcase?" I just helped her into the car.

Six hours later, Peter Joseph Wolfinger the Third was born. We named him Peter after my grandfather and Joseph after my father-in-law. When I able to see Judy, she smiled and said, "Happy Birthday." I hugged and kissed her.

"Thank you," I said. "He was some present."

She said, "Yes, and he weighs 9 lbs, 13 ounces." She asked me to pull the curtain around us, which I did. She said, "Come close." She opened her robe and said, "Look good. Kiss them goodbye. I'm taking these pills to shrink them, and our son is coming home on baby formula." Then we laughed. I hugged and kissed her again. I told her they were fun while they lasted, and Judy just said, "So you say."

After the christening, everything went back to routine. Silver loved little Peter; Judy was busy being a mother and housewife, and I was working.

CHAPTER 40

It was a Saturday, and I was getting ready to take Judy food shopping when the doorbell rang. I answered the door to see Dave standing there. Behind him, there was a U-Haul truck. He hugged me and said, "I'm going to miss you. Please, help me move."

I said, "What are you talking about?"

He said, "I went hunting in Massachusetts. I love it up there, so I'm moving up there."

I said, "What about a job? What did Maddy say? Are you nuts, you have a good job?"

Dave said, "I don't care. I need to get out of here. Let's go."

I told Judy, and we followed Dave in our car. When we went up to his apartment, Maddy was sitting on the couch, feeding the baby.

Dave said, "We are moving now. Pack up everything, and let's go."

Maddy said, "What? Are you crazy?"

Dave said, "Come or stay, but we're moving."

Maddy gave little Dave to Judy to hold, called her mother to tell her the news, and then started packing. Once they were packed, Dave hugged me and said, "I will miss you. Come see us." Then he jumped into the truck and left.

Judy turned to me and said, "I would kill you if you did that to me."

I said, "I would never, but Dave has been troubled since we came home. Only, he can work it out."

Two months went by when I got a phone call from Maddy, crying and saying that Dave had no job wouldn't take help from her family. She said they were starving. I said, "Give me the address." I then called the office asked for two vacation days, asked Judy to pack a bag, and told her, "We will be gone for a few days." I then explained what happened.

When we got to Chicopee Falls, we went over a wooden bridge and found ourselves in a small town; it still had horse-hitching posts out front of the stores. We stopped at a super market, and we bought canned foods and other items that could stretch a meal. Judy took out small bills and put them in her pocket to slip to Maddy.

We arrived at the house, which looked like a three-floor World War II barrack. When we got there, Dave was working on his truck and was surprised to see us. He came over and hugged us while asking what we were doing there. I opened the trunk and said, "Just saying hello and bringing you a welcome to Massachusetts gift. Now help me bring this into your place."

He said, "I'm not taking handouts."

I said, "Remember when I was so sick I couldn't get out of my cot from malaria? You got me to medic and got me fresh fruit from who knows where. Well this is pay back. You don't want it? Starve. This is for little Dave and Maddy."

Dave just smiled and started helping carry all the packages up to the third floor while telling me he had been putting food on the table by hunting. He also told me he was starting a job next week.

Judy told them we were treating them for dinner. We must have driven for an hour in the dark when we finally saw a very large sign ahead with lots of cars around the building. All sorts of people were there. Dave said, "This is the only place to go." We parked the car. The girls went for the food, and while they were gone, I turned to Dave and asked why he was doing this. He replied, "Pete, you and I are cut from two different cloths. Remember when we were in the jungle, you had a hard time wiping your ass with a leaf? Well, I grew up that way. Or when we had camp-out houses? That was a step up for me. I grew up planting food and killing animals so we could eat. I tried your way of life; the men laugh at my accent. They would joke behind my back about how I dress. Then Maddy's family made her an outcast for marrying me. I just had to get away. I know it is tough for Maddy, but me, I'm at home. I promised myself I will always put my family first. I looked down to see his feet were wrapped in black tape.

I said, "Dave, I know I have a horseshoe up my ass. Now let me share some of my luck. Here is 200 dollars; buy shoes, so you can go to work, and clothes for yourself, and when you get on your feet, pay me back. This is between you and me as brothers. Please don't say no. I hate to have a fist fight over money." With tears in our eyes, we said "brothers forever."

The girls returned and said, "What are you two doing?"

I replied, "Just telling jokes." That was a night I'll always remember. And he did pay me back.

CHAPTER 41

The year was 1974. I was a lead mechanic, had my own truck and a helper; life was great. One night, I was in bed, who knows what I was thinking, when I heard Judy say, "Do you like?" I opened my eyes to see Judy standing there in only baby blue bikini panties with mesh lace on the front. My answer came nine months later when Joseph was born. With Judy being pregnant, the house was too small. So, we started talking of moving, but we didn't know where to move.

One night I pulled up to our house to see Judy's family and mine with the police. I ran in and asked, "What happened?" All the women were upstairs with Judy. While the police were finishing the paper work, I asked again what had happened. My father and father-in-law told me the following:

Judy took Peter Jr. to the store. On the way back, a man approached her and asked if he could come home with her and show her books that he was selling. She said no, thanking him and continuing on her way home. Once in the house, she turned to see the man trying to come in; she was able to lock the door just in time. Then she saw the man run to the back to open the rear door. She took Peter and ran upstairs, locking the bedroom door. Then, she called the police, my father, and her father. When they got there, the back door was open, and there were pieces of clothing and blood on the floor. They believed the man had opened the back door and met Silver. From the blood and clothing, they believed Silver severely bit him in a few places; they found traces of blood leaving the house and going to the back fence.

I went upstairs to see my mother holding Peter and my mother-in-law holding Judy. I said, "Judy, are you alright?" She shook her head yes, and I asked, "Do you want a doctor?"

She said no. After everyone left, Judy and I laid in bed. I let her cry. She looked at me and said, "Why is it always me? There are prettier and better built girls out there than me."

I said, "The best way I can explain it is put Ann-Margret and Marilyn Monroe together, in the same clothes and hair style, and ask a man to choose one. 99 percent of the men will choose Marilyn over Ann, even though Ann is just as beautiful and built just as nicely as Marilyn."

Judy said, "Why?"

I said, "Marilyn radiates sex, even if she doesn't want to. Even when she wears her reading glasses, she looks sexy, and you my love do the same, radiate sex. Whether you want to or not. I cannot tell you how many of my friends say I'm a lucky bastard after they see and meet you."

She said, "No Pete, I'm the lucky one."

Before she fell asleep, I called the office and said I wasn't coming in the next day.

The next day I put dead bolts on all the doors and set up a leash attached to the baby carriage, so Silver could walk with her when she went out. The family checked in on her, and everything went back to normal for the moment. Every weekend we would look at houses on Long Island; each weekend we went a little farther out. We finally found our house and were getting ready to move when Judy started getting obscene phone calls. We called the police and were told get a whistle and blow into the phone every time the man called.

I bought a whistle for her and told our families what was happening. One day my Aunt Lilly was with Judy when he called; my Aunt Lilly grabbed the phone and told him come over and let her show him what a real woman can do. He hung up; he didn't call for a while, then started again. Judy started blowing the whistle, and the calls stopped. We moved two weeks after our son, Joseph, was born.

CHAPTER 42

I now joined the commuter gang and started to learn what living in the suburbs was like. Everywhere you had to go, you needed a car. We decided for Judy to keep the good car, and I would get a cheap car to commute in. I was lucky to find a couple of guys from my department that lived near me, so we would meet at a location and commute together. The hardest part was trying to line up overtime for all of us. The rule was the driver could not work overtime if the rest of us couldn't.

The next problem was getting a veteran's tax break, so I went to the veterans' office. They looked up my record and asked why I didn't apply for a disability for my foot. I said, "Why would I do that? How could I look a brother veteran who lost an arm in the face and tell him I was wounded too, in the big toe, by a 105 shell?"

He handed me the paper to sign while saying, "Give it a try." Then he said, "If you go to college, the government would pay you 600 dollars a month if you take 12 credits."

I said, "I will think about it," and left.

That night I told Judy what was offered to me as a veteran. She said, "Why not go?"

I said, "Because it would mean you would have to do everything because I would never be home."

She replied, "You should go."

I said, "I'll think about it."

The following week Matt and John were severely burnt from an explosion. Matt was going up the ladder when the primary let go and blew him out of the hole. John was on top and the explosion caught him in the face. They were bought to the burn unit in Manhattan; the company asked for volunteers to drive their wives back and forth to the hospital. We would be paid straight time only. I drew night shift. I would just sit out in the car and wait. Sometimes the wives would go and sometimes not. This went on for a month, then the company said it was cheaper for the wives to call a cab, and the company would reimburse them.

One day the wife of Jim (my car pool partner) was talking to Judy on the phone about the accident and told her, "Jim said Wolfie has a horseshoe up his ass because he was on his way to relieve Matt."

That night after dinner, Judy put the boys to bed and came in to sit down next to me in the den. I could see her eyes sparkle like diamonds, which meant to me that she was mad. I had already gotten the feeling that she was angry at dinner. I looked at her and asked what was wrong. She said, "When were you going to tell me it could have been you?"

I said, "What? Who told you that?"

She replied, "Jim's wife, Sue."

I said, "And what do you want me to do?"

She replied, "Go to college."

I said, "You realize that I will leave 5:45 a.m. and be back home at 11 p.m., 6 days a week, all year long. Meaning that you must handle everything."

She said, "Yes, and it's better than losing you."

I said, "OK, let's give it a try."

CHAPTER 43

In September 1976, I started college, and June 1978, I graduated college with an associate's degree. The Veterans Department was giving scholarships. I told Judy, and she told me to take the test. I did and received one year free for any college of my choice. I talked it over with Judy, and she said, "Go for it." I said, "It will be another two years of you doing everything."

She put her arms around me and said, "If it will keep you safe, I'll do 40 years." Then she kissed me.

I said, "Hey, are you just trying to keep me out of the house?"

Laughing, she said, "I'll show you tonight how much I miss you."

I started Dowling College in September 1978 and graduated June 1980 with a Bachelor of Science degree. Judy gave me a graduation party and invited our families, friends, and neighbors. My good friend and neighbor, Paul, and I were sitting on our lounge chairs talking when Judy said, "Attention everyone. This is my present to Pete." There was a large object in the center of the patio with a large cover over. I got up, walked over to the object, and pulled the cover off. It was our lawn mower, with a large sign on it, which read in big letters "YOUR TURN NOW." Everyone laughed.

I walked back and sat back down with Paul; he said to me, "I'm going to miss her mowing the lawn.

I replied, "It might be safer for you."

Paul looked at me and said, "Are you jealous?"

I said, "No. I saw you go to open your door at the same time Judy bent over. That door hit you so hard you looked like a walking drunk for a few moments."

Paul asked, "You saw that?"

I said, "Yup. I laughed for days."

Paul said, "Why aren't you jealous?"

"When I was very young, I learned that if a woman does not want to stay with you, there is nothing in the world you can do to keep her, and I know

I have Judy's heart. Don't get me wrong, I would kill the man that would try to take her from me against her will, and she knows that," I responded. "You have a pretty wife. Do you get jealous?"

Paul said, "I love Kathy and yes, she is pretty, and I do get jealous at times. But with you and Judy there is something that is different. When Judy looks at you, she smiles, and her face lights up."

I said, "Like Beauty and the Beast."

Paul thought for a moment then agreed, "Yes, that's it."

I said, "Fuck you." We both laughed.

The rest of the night was beautiful. After everyone left and the kids were in bed, Judy said to me, "Now for your real present."

CHAPTER 44

I stayed in the union until July of 1983, when I took a position for a foreman's job in the Astoria transformer shop. The position was outside of my department, which I wanted. I was offered management positions within my department, but I felt I would be put in an awkward position, knowing what I know about all the dark secrets of the men I worked beside for years, so I turned them down, which did not make management happy.

The day I left, my partner said, "Remember, you cannot eat a title. Are you sure?"

I said, "Jim, just knowing I don't have to grow a beard every winter, having regular hours, and performing no more back-breaking work makes this worth it."

And he never spoke truer words, but my word to Judy was more than money could buy, so I thought.

The first few months were tough. My raise for a year is what I would earn in a month in overtime in the union, but Judy was happy. She was always smiling, even though she would say we were never so poor since I went into management. Because of my degree and knowledge, I was in charge of the production and reconditioning of the network protector (large circuit breaker). Money was tight, but Judy never complained, which bothered me. I hated not having enough money for what we needed, and I hated credit cards, so things were getting tight. Then one day, I was talking to my friend, Fred, about the financial situation; he suggested that I join the United States Coast Guard Reserves. I asked him what that was, and he explained, "I joined. We meet once a month and two weeks a year, and we get 200 dollars a month. The company also pays us the difference in our pay."

I said, "Let me talk it over with Judy."

Fred said, "Call me."

I agreed.

It was hard getting used to being home early, and a lot of the time the boys definitely seemed unhappy. I had a feeling Judy was not telling me every-thing that was going on in our house. I mean nothing bad, just the boys misbehaving and begging Judy not to tell me so I wouldn't punish them. All children have the standard saying, "Mom, please mom, don't tell Dad."

A surprise came when I got home early. Judy was out with the boys shop-ping. It was Friday. I went to the mailbox and gathered the mail. While go-ing through the mail, I saw a check for $60 from the VA. I thought, "Wow, I guess they approved my injury." I took the check and went to the bank.

When I gave the check to the teller, the teller said, "Please see the manger to approve this check." I asked her why, but she just said, "Please follow me," and lead me to the manager's office.

Upon entering the office, the manager asked me to sit down. Then she said, "Mr. Wolfinger, do you have an ID?"

As I gave her my ID, I asked, "Is there a problem?"

She replied, "Mr. Wolfinger, your wife has been coming in cashing this monthly check for over a year, and the signatures are different."

I said, "Oh, thank you. May I have the check back, so I get this straighten out with my wife."

She handed me the check and said, "Please do. We are always here to help."

When I got home, Judy was putting the groceries away with Joseph, who was 9 at the time, helping. When they saw me, their faces lit up. Judy smiled and said, "I see you're home early. Isn't it nice to be home early and have dinner with us?"

Joseph said, "Dad, a man was looking at mommy, so I said out loud, 'Daddy is home lifting weights.' Right mom?"

Judy smiled and said, "Yes, my protector."

I said, "Joseph, go to the other room and play. Daddy wants to talk to Mom." Once he left the kitchen, I held up the check and said, "Well, when were you going to tell me about this?"

She walked over smiling and took the check while saying, "This is mine for putting you through college and fighting to make sure you have a safe job." I quickly grabbed her around the waist, pulling her close to me; Silver quickly stood up.

I said, "Silver sit. I knew her before you." I pulled her closer to me and said, "What do I get?"

She smiled, kissed me, and said, "Me and dinner, and if you're really good, maybe, dessert tonight. Now go wash your hands."

That evening I told Judy that I was going to join the Coast Guard. She immediately asked what it was and if it was dangerous. I proceeded to explain everything, concluding "In the end, it is not dangerous."

CHAPTER 45

That Saturday, Fred and I went out to the Shinnecock Base and I was sworn in. As long as I stayed at E-4 rank and my disability did not go over 10 percent, I was good. I was assigned to the Shinnecock Base, which was search-and-rescue base.

Fred was right, it was nice. We rode around in a 44-foot boat, doing boat inspections, or sitting in class learning. We did a few rescues, which consisted mostly of people not paying attention to warnings. When a call came out for help, the crew was always asked as volunteers. I never saw any boat crew member refuse. Most of the rescues were on nice days, but some were not; it was the luck of the draw. When you were a weekend reservist, the rule was, the reserves report and the regulars leave. In order to be a coxswain (boat operator), you first had to know the local waters; I was studying them when a call came in that a small yacht was sinking and the weather was getting rough. When we got there, the yacht was sinking; we sent a monkey fist (a rope shot from a 22 rifle with a big ball on the end to give it weight). The man on the boat did not know what to do. I gave the helm to the coxswain and instructed him to get me close. When we were close, I jumped on board; the water was already on deck, so we had to work fast. I tied the rope to the opposite side of the yacht, bringing our boat close. I helped the man, wife, and children onto our boat, then I jumped on and cut the rope. We had just got on the Coast Guard vessel when the yacht sunk. The man couldn't stop thanking all of us and said he was going to write the commander.

One day I came home to find Judy crying, so I said, "What happened?"

She threw a letter from the Coast Guard at me, saying, "You lied to me. You said it wasn't dangerous." The letter said our boat crew would be getting a letter of commendation for saving the lives of the Vice President of Dime Savings Bank and his family while risking their own lives.

I put the letter down and said, "I wasn't in danger; they were."

She said, "Don't pull that shit.

"OK," I responded. "I can't quit, but I will transfer to GI (Governors Island) where we just do port inspections on land."

She said, "Don't lie to me."

I said, "I'm not. Besides, men would be lined up to marry you, and you would be rich."

She flew off the chair and started to hit me while yelling "I love you, you jerk, and I was trying to get you away from doing all this dangerous shit." She grabbed her car keys and got ready to leave. She then said, "I'm taking the boys to my mother's. Make your own dinner."

Truth be told, I had never seen her so mad. That night when I was getting ready to go to bed, Judy came in, and her eyes still looked like diamonds, which meant that I was still in hot water. I said, "Judy, I'm sorry."

Before I could say anything else, she said, "Stop." Then Judy said, "Pete, do you think I'm stupid?"

I said, "No."

"Do you think I don't know men look at me?"

I said, "No."

"Did you ever see me look at another man?"

I said, "No."

"Do you think I love you?"

I said, "Yes."

"Do you think that if I didn't love you, I would stay with you?"

I said, "No."

She said, "You hurt me tonight, really bad. I will forgive you this time, but never say that again to me."

I said, "I promise."

She came over, kissed me with tears in her eyes, and said, "Good night. I'm going downstairs to watch TV."

I never felt as bad as I did that night. The following month I reported to GI and joined the Port Security Unit; our main task was to inspect all facilities that contain hazards that may enter the waterways, for example oil refineries. The unit was all reserves, and 99 percent of them were cops and firemen; 1 percent was Con Edison, including me. They were a great group and accepted me as a brother.

CHAPTER 46

It was August 1990. We were in our office working when Joe C. told me he had been activated for Desert Shield and this would be his last day working before reporting to his Army station. From there, they would be sending his unit over to Iraq.

I replied, "You should've listened to me, Joe, and gone into the Coast Guard Reserves instead of the Army Reserves."

As he was leaving, Joe hollered out, "Don't worry, Wolfie, you'll be joining me." Laughing, he headed toward his car.

I said to myself, "Not me. I already spent 11 months and 29 days in a living hell called Vietnam."

Before you knew it, it was January 1991. Desert Shield turned into Desert Storm, and the war was just beginning. That night in January, I felt secure that I was not going to end up alone sleeping on a cot and fighting for my life like the last war I was in.

I woke up feeling the warmth of my beautiful wife's body next to mine. The scent of her awakened my manhood. I rolled over, gently kissed her, and brought her body closer to me, only to hear the words, "You know we can't. The kids are here in the next room."

I answered, "Who said 'Let's have kids?'" We laughed as she turned over and went back to sleep. As I was dressing, I could hear her breathing as she slept. Not wanting to wake her again, I left for work.

Getting into my jeep, I recalled that since this was Martin Luther King Jr. Day and just a few of us were working, it should be a nice quiet day. An hour and a half later, I parked my jeep and headed into my office.

As I passed my fellow worker, John hollered, "Heard from Joe C. He is now in the largest sand pit. Iraq!"

My reply was "Yeah. I told him not to join the Army Reserves. I said he should join the Coast Guard Reserves as I did. Now, he's sleeping in and eating sand, and I'm sleeping in a nice warm bed." As I continued walking toward my office, the secretary's phone rang. I picked it up and heard a voice say, "May I please speak to Petty Officer Peter Wolfinger."

I replied, "This is Petty Officer Peter Wolfinger speaking."

The voice on the other end said, "This is Lieutenant Johnson of the United States Coast Guard. You are hereby activated until further notice. You have 24 hours to report to Governors Island."

My response was, "Well, I'm the Admiral of the United States Coast Guard."

Lieutenant Johnson replied, "This is no joke. If you say that again, you will spend the rest of your life in the brig."

"Sorry, sir, I thought you were my friend playing a joke on me."

Lieutenant Johnson replied, "Any questions, Petty Officer?"

"I'm 40 years old. Don't you think that's kind old to be activated?"

Lieutenant Johnson replied, "I have your entire record in front of me, including your tour in Vietnam. For what we want you for, you are perfect."

"What about my civilian job?"

Lieutenant Johnson replied, "As we speak, the orders are being sent to your office. Report to Governors Island tomorrow morning at 8 a.m. sharp." Then, he hung up.

I stood there looking at the phone in my hand and saying to myself, "What the hell just happened?" Then I heard the fax machine start up. I turned around to see papers from the Coast Guard coming through.

I picked up my papers, made a copy, and then gave a copy to John before I headed toward the door.

John hollered out, "Where you going?"

"Read the papers."

As I drove home, I was trying to figure out how to tell Judy and the children. When I walked through the door, Judy was doing the wash, and the children were outside playing.

Judy saw me and looked surprised. "What are you doing home so early?"

"I don't want you to get upset now, but I've been activated into the Coast Guard."

She stood still, like she did not believe what she was hearing; then tears started to roll down her cheeks. I took her into my arms and hugged her, telling her not to worry. It's the Coast Guard not the Army. I will call the first chance I can." Then I went upstairs and packed my sea bag.

The next morning as I was coming down the steps, Judy was in the hallway, waiting for me with tears in her eyes. I again told her not to worry. "I will call the first chance I get," I repeated. "Tell the children I love them."

She walked me to my jeep. I put my sea bag in the rear of the vehicle. We hugged and kissed one more time before I left for Governors Island.

CHAPTER 47

As I drove toward Governors Island, I began having flashbacks of the things I did in Vietnam. My mind was full of a lot of memories that I was hoping to forget. Before I knew it, I was on a ferry heading toward Governors Island. I parked my jeep and headed for the school auditorium. As I entered the auditorium, I saw many familiar faces of fellow reservists that I had been drilling with each month over the years.

Once we were all inside the auditorium, the officer in charge said, "Attention. All personnel sit down except for the following 12 names. These personnel will report to the church."

As luck would have it, I was one of the 12. The 12 of us headed toward the church, not knowing what to expect. Once we entered the church, we were instructed to stand for roll call. When that finished, we were told to sit down.

The commander stood in the church pulpit. He stated the following, "You have all been activated because of Desert Storm and what we are telling you is highly classified. You are not to tell anyone, including your family. You have all been cleared for this mission. There will be a team of 12 with no rank on collars, no saying rate. You will only be addressed as Petty Officer and will only wear your work blues and a white helmet. When traveling to your destination, your transportation will be three black, unmarked Chevrolet Suburbans. Now take your sea bags and report to the senior chief outside."

We put the sea bags in the rear of the Suburbans, then we climbed into the trucks and headed to our destination. Everyone was quiet. We were all deep in our own thoughts.

We drove for about two hours, and it was dark by the time we reached our destination, a Coast Guard base somewhere in New Jersey. We were stopped at the gate where the guard checked the paperwork then instructed us to continue to the rear of the compound.

The Suburbans drove to the rear of the compound and parked in front of a building that looked like World War II barracks. A senior chief told us to take our sea bags, go up to the second floor, and meet in the large break room. When we got to the second floor, it was dark, and we fumbled around to find some lighting.

Once someone found the lights and turned them on, we observed white iron beds with rolled up mattresses. The team members explored the rest of the floor and found about six separate rooms, so we decided to split up into the separate rooms and use the main room as a dayroom. We ran the plan by the senior chief, and he was OK with the plan, but he wanted his own room, which worked out well.

Once we were all settled in, we discovered an old TV in a corner. Joe turned it on, and to our surprise it worked! One of the team said, "Let's all chip in and get cable!" We all agreed. A more thorough inspection of the room and adjacent rooms revealed a couple of beat-up couches.

John said, "Wow. This isn't going to be too bad. Now we just have to find out what are we going to do."

It was getting toward chow time, and all of us were hungry, so we told the chief that we were going to head toward the mess hall. The senior chief said he would meet us there later.

As we headed toward the mess hall, we joked about our assignments, mused about what they might be, and wondered how long we would be away from our loved ones. We did know we were activated for Desert Storm, but we didn't know why or for how long.

We also knew it was January, and we were freezing our balls off as we headed toward the mess hall. We arrived at the mess just as dinner started. We joined the line after all of the regulars had been served. Then, the mess chief stepped in front of us and stated that, as we were out of uniform, he was not going to serve us in his mess hall.

Stunned we turned around and were heading out of the mess hall when we met the senior chief coming in. We told him what happened with the mess chief. His face turned red with anger. "Turn around and follow me!" he ordered.

So, we walked back into the mess hall with the senior chief in the lead. The mess chief saw us coming and said, "I told you no food."

The senior chief took out his ID card and showed the card to the mess chief while stating, "Read my ID!"

The mess chief replied, "It says senior chief."

The senior chief replied, "That is correct. Never question me or any of my men again, or we can go to the old man. You're supposed to check ID cards. Not appearances! We are assigned here until further notice, and you will be serving us. You are not to ask questions. I expect you to have food for my team when we enter your mess. Do we understand each other, Chief?"

"Yes," replied the chief as he turned to his team and instructed them to give us sandwiches. We all sat down and started to eat the sandwiches like we had never eaten before.

We were tired, hungry, curious, and anxious to start our assignments. The next morning, we got up at 0600, dressed, and headed for the chow hall where we had a quick breakfast before we jumped into our black trucks and followed the senior chief to our destination.

We arrived at the front gate of a facility and were met there by armed guards. They inspected all our ID cards and allowed us through. We rode about 2 miles before we got to a wooden bridge. The bridge had railroad tracks that stretched straight out to the ocean. We rode this bridge for 3 miles. I thought to myself, "This doesn't look too good." There were no lights and no guardrails, so we rode in the center of the railroad track, heading toward the sea. And I didn't see any end to the track.

About 20 minutes later, we arrived at what looked like a main birthing area for vessels. We all piled out of the cars and headed to the main building as the senior chief had instructed us to do. It was a cold day, even for such a short walk, and we froze by the time we got to the building.

Once in the building, we removed our coats, sat down, and waited, not knowing what to expect. About 15 minutes later, a man entered the room and introduced himself as Ron. Ron was in charge of loading a variety of equipment, and he was in charge of the piers.

Ron brought in a blackboard that showed various boxes with names on them and an image of a model container ship. He stated that we would all start loading explosives onto container ships immediately after this meeting. We were to be broken up into three teams, each consisting of four men. Our job was to oversee the loading of these explosives without any issues!

Should we see any problems, we were to stop all operations until the problem was resolved. All the stevedores (persons the load and unload cargo) would be Army personnel with no rate, and they were instructed to listen to our instructions once we started loading. We would be identified by our white hats. We were given a vessel inspection form that would be filled out by us prior to loading the explosives. Our fork trucks would be electric. Brass nails and hammers were the only tools to be used to reinforce the cases of explosives. Phosphate would always be placed in the lowest hole of the ship. Should there be a problem, the phosphate would burn a hole through the hull of the ship and send it to the bottom.

We were instructed that should we hear three whistles, we should stop all operations and report immediately to the main area on the piers for a head count.

The senior chief stepped forward and designated how the 12 men would be broken into three teams. "First team: John, Mike, George, Mario. Second team: Bob, Tony, Ralph, Sal. Third team: Wolfie, Freddie, Wayne, Charlie."

He continued, "Because of the cold weather and the fact that you will be standing on top of the hatches most of the time, I will relieve each of you, one at a time, for 20 minutes. The first ship is now here and docked. Team one is up. The second ship will arrive at 0900 when team two is up. At 10:00 the third ship will arrive when team three is up.

"It will take approximately 18 hours to load each ship, and we will not stop except for lightning. You will see the Army stevedores change shift every four hours, but that does not apply to you. Any questions?" He took a brief pause, "Good. Teams two and three will return to base, relax, and get ready."

CHAPTER 48

The next morning, team two went to the docks while the rest of us just stayed in the barracks.

Toward the end of January, we were informed that we could call home and write, but we were not to say *where* we were or what we were doing.

The days were long, and the weather was brutal.

Once, as we were loading a vessel from Germany, a man fell overboard. I called to "Cease Operations" and prepared to go into rescue mode when I was instructed to continue operations and that the divers would retrieve the body. Because we had so many clothes on due to the severe cold weather, it was determined that should anyone fall overboard, the weight of his clothes would take that person directly to the bottom like an anchor.

I made a note to myself not to walk too close to the edge and not to fall over when loading barges.

The weather was not cooperating, but as fast as the ships came in, we loaded them and sent them back out.

One night in January, the dock master said, "We have to load all the ships tonight and get these explosives out immediately, but I'm not sure if I want to give that approval. This is the roughest weather we have had. It's 20 degrees with strong winds, making the ocean spray feel like icy rain."

While discussing this, word came from above to load. "They need these explosives, so start loading now," hollered the senior chief.

My team went to the ship called *Pride,* and as we boarded the vessel, it was so cold that when the waves hit the side of the ship, the ocean spray felt like ice cubes, and it quickly turned the deck into an ice rink. Everybody was sliding all over, trying to hold on.

We were able to open up the first three hatches. The plan was to stay with the crew in the hold and watch from there. There was no phosphate this time; we were loading the explosives. The ship was rocking, but the crews seemed to go with the rocking. Then, out of the blue, a rogue wave hit the side of the ship really hard, knocking pallets and shells to the floor, breaking some of the bombs open, and spilling powder all over the deck.

The next second, I heard the crew screaming, "We're all going to die!" They started scrambling up the ladder and climbing up the sides of the wall and bulkhead. They were going as fast as their feet could carry them. At the same time, I heard someone scream, "HELP!"

I looked around and saw the fork truck driver looking like he was in shock. I yelled at him, "Don't move!" After scanning the area, I identified the problem. The fork truck was sitting on top of two damaged bombs. I explained to the driver that we would have to remove the shells from underneath his truck, but first I would need to secure the truck to prevent it from moving.

Then, I had to remove the bombs.

In order to do this, I had to stick my hands under the fork truck and pull out the two damaged bombs. I instructed the driver to keep his foot on the brake and to say a prayer. I started to move the bombs. I tried to distract him by talking to him about his family and reassuring him that in a few seconds it would all be over. During this time, the ship was still rocking, but thankfully not as hard.

We could hear the sirens blasting and people hollering and running around. I kept talking to the driver as I gently pulled on the bombs. I could feel the gunpowder grinding into my hands, but I kept moving gently and slowly pulling the bombs out. At the time, I forgot that I had gloves in my pockets

It felt like years, even though I knew it had been only seconds, minutes at most. After I removed the second bomb, I cleaned the area by the wheels of gun powder and put the chock in back of the wheels. Once that was done, I instructed the driver that he could now leave, but he had to walk very carefully. He moved out so fast, I thought he was running on air.

After he left, I surveyed the area and started to stabilize the bombs. The bomb team arrived, and I was told to leave which I had no problem doing. I asked the senior chief if I could go back to base. He said, "Sure. I will drive you."

On the way back to base we sat in silence for a while, then he said, "I'm going to put you in for a medal. It was a brave thing you did."

I thanked him. The rest of the ride back we sat in silence, each caught up in our own thoughts.

The next morning, I woke up with blisters on my hands, but I didn't think anything of it. I put my gloves on and went back to work with my team. When I got back to the docks, there were all new workers. I asked the senior chief, "Where is the old crew?"

He told me that they were all traumatized, so they were dismissed and sent home. I asked, "What about me?"

"What about you?" The senior chief replied sarcastically.

"Can't I go home?" I inquired.

The senior chief said, "No, you didn't look traumatized enough." He instructed me to take the third hatch, and then he left.

The following morning, I woke up and my hands were hurting really bad. The blisters had doubled in size and were starting to break open.

When the senior chief saw my hands, he said, "That doesn't look good. Let's go to the medical office on Governors Island." We went to a small medical office on Governors Island instead of the hospital because of our need for secrecy.

The medical staff said they looked like acid burns, and they wanted to know where I got them. I told them I had no idea, so they cleaned the blisters, put ointment on them, and bandaged my hands. They gave me some extra ointment and bandages and instructed me to change them daily.

The senior chief later gave me copies of the medical report, as well as the letter he submitted for a medal, and instructed me to keep them. "You never can tell when you might need them."

A few days or maybe a week later, the captain requested that the chief and I report back to Governors Island for a meeting. The captain explained why the medal would not be issued. He stated that in the best interest of our nation this incident never happened. All documentation of that day would be removed. The captain apologized and then dismissed us.

It was now the end of January, and according to the news, the war was over, but we were still loading our own ships and barges, as well as ships from all over the world. The conflict may have been over, yet we continued to work quickly and efficiently.

CHAPTER 49

By the end of February, the arrival of the ships started to slow, and we found we had extra time for ourselves. We couldn't go home because we were on call 24/7.

By April, we started to put our sweats on and go for a jog every day. Our base was located in a park called Sandy Hook. We would jog around the Sandy Hook peninsula from which we could actually see the loading docks.

All of my fellow Coasties were fireman, except for me. I never really knew why and how I was assigned to the group. They broke my balls in a friendly way. In the beginning they would drag me out of bed to go jogging. I would holler, "I don't have to run up stairs to save people."

They would laugh and continue to pull me out of bed as they teased, "But you have to run when your customers see their electric bill!"

Since the ships were now arriving with less frequency, we made a team chart schedule, so when a ship did arrive at the dock, we knew which team was up.

We were also allowed off base but could not go far. When we had time off, we would go to the local area bar and grill, called the Hideaway. The bar was located underneath the bridge that went to Sandy Hook, and we often saw the bar's lights when coming back from our night shift.

We lucked out. The bar served good food and cold drinks and had good music. It was more of a local's bar than a tourist place. I must say, it was nice to relax and talk to each other about the day's events and life in general. Normally, we would just sit in the truck, go back to base, take a shower, and fall in the bed or hang out in the day room.

We stayed to ourselves and did not mingle with our fellow Coasties on the base or anyone off base. When we did meet others, we would say "Hello," then continue on our way without starting a conversation. Every morning we started each new day all over again.

The months went by fast and before we knew it, it was June, and they were opening up the Sandy Hook beaches. Traffic was heavy, but we had special privileges. Our trucks were jet black with blackout windows, and when needed to, we used flashing lights, so we were able to run on the side of the road, passing the heavy traffic going to the beach.

Every Wednesday and Saturday night they had singers at the Sandy Hook Restaurant. The stage was huge, and you could see the singers from the top of an off-road dune. We found a pretty good spot to park our black trucks on top of the hill. Looking down from that position, we were able to see the singers on stage performing, and no one noticed us, except those who were on stage.

CHAPTER 50

One morning I woke up very early, got dressed in my summer blues, and headed for the front door. Fred hollered out, "Don't know where you're going so early. Don't care. Just make sure you're back for 1200 formation."

I waved the "OK" sign so not to wake anyone and headed out the front door. As I was heading toward the front gate, I went to a pay phone and called for a cab. By the time I got to the front gate, the cab was waiting. The guards knew us all by now and waved me through.

The sun just came up as I was crossing the street to the car. I heard a garbage truck coming up the block. I turned to look at the truck, not seeing a car weaving down the road.

Before I knew it, I was lying on the ground. When I looked up all I saw was a pair of beautiful legs and pink panties and I heard, "Oh, my God. Oh, my God! What did I do? Are you all right?"

As I was trying to gather my senses, my eyes were moving up and looking at a very pretty woman, who was now on her knees crying. I got up to brush myself off and help her up. "I'm OK," I said.

She replied, "Thank God" and then passed out.

You could smell the alcohol all over her. I gently picked her up and put her in the car. I tried to wake her up, but she was out cold. I looked around for an address, but I could not find anything. I checked the GPS, which was getting popular at that time, and found where she lived. I drove the car to the house, pulled into the driveway, and parked. Looking in her pocket-book, I found her keys and opened the door. I carried her inside and laid her down on the couch.

I left and shut the door. I walked down the driveway and headed toward the nearest intersection where I called another cab and headed back to base. I made it just in time for the 1200 formation. I still don't understand why we had to be in dress uniform just for the commander to inspect his men, but that is the military life. After inspection, we all went to the Sandy Hook Restaurant instead of the Hideaway because it was closer to base. We stayed to ourselves, had a few drinks, and then went back to base.

CHAPTER 51

The following morning, Sarah opened her eyes when she heard the front door open as the maid Molly came in. "Good morning, Ms. Russo," Molly said. "How are you feeling? Looks like you had a rough night."

"Yes. I did. I drank way too much. I had this dream that I hit a soldier with my car, and I don't remember how I even got here."

As she got off the couch, she told Molly, "I'm going to take a shower, get dressed, and then go to town to get my nails done." Once dressed, she grabbed her keys and pocket book. She hollered, "So long, Molly," and headed toward her car.

She could not shake the feeling that she had hit someone the previous night, so she walked around the car, but she did not see anything out of the ordinary. "Probably a bad dream," she said to herself as she opened the car door, slid inside, put the key in the ignition, and started the car. When she moved her foot, she felt something on the floor. Looking down, she picked up a cluster of different colored ribbons. She placed it in her pocket and continued to the nail salon before heading to work at the restaurant where she sang.

While getting dressed for rehearsal, she decided she would call Jeff Half who owned an investigation company and see if he could make any sense out of the ribbons she found in her car. She asked Jeff if he would meet her for lunch at the restaurant.

Over lunch, Sarah explained how she found the ribbons in her car but couldn't recall what happened that night, as everything was a burr. Jeff examined the ribbons. "These tell a story of a person who is in the Coast Guard. Someone who has seen combat and has quite a few other metals that I am not familiar with." Jeff put the ribbons into his pocket. "Is there anything else that you remember? Anything?"

"I vaguely remember seeing a man who was tall. He was wearing a light blue shirt and a nice smile."

Jeff replied, "That's a pretty good start for now. Do you think you would remember him if you saw him again?"

"I believe I would," she replied.

Jeff stood up. "I'll see what I can find out."

Jeff was familiar with the local area. After reviewing the medal, he noted some were Coast Guard medals, and he knew that there was a Coast Guard base in Sandy Hook Park. He would start there. He knew he could not get onto the base, so he sat in his car and snapped pictures of men coming out of the base. This got very boring. The most exciting thing on the radio was the news that Sammy the Bull had died and no one knew why. Now, Anthony Zito would be set free because Sammy could no longer testify against him.

Every once in a while, Jeff would see a black Chevy Suburban with no markings drive out of the base. Although unusual, that was not what he was there for. After a few days he was about to give up when the gate opened and 10 to 12 men came out and started jogging through the park. Jeff began snapping pictures of each man as they were jogging, hoping that one might be the man Sarah was looking for.

Jeff watched for a few more days to make sure it was routine for the joggers to come out every day at about the same time. Jeff called Sarah and said he may have something; he arranged for them to meet the next day for lunch at the Sandy Hook Restaurant.

Jeff ordered a beer and ham sandwich as Sarah reviewed the photographs. Suddenly, Sarah jumped up from the table, almost spilling Jeff's beer. "The tall guy, he looks very familiar."

Jeff replied, "Now, it's up to you. My job is done. I recommend that you wait outside the gate. When they come out, you can join the group when they are jogging and get a closer look."

"I will do that." Replied Sarah

The following morning, Sarah was so excited that she got up really early, dressed in her jogging gear, jumped in her car, and drove to the front gate of the base, where she waited for the joggers. Finally, they came out and started jogging toward the park. Sarah got out of her car and started jogging behind them. Soon she was up next to the tall guy.

"Good morning," Sarah said to the tall jogger.

"Good morning," he replied.

As they were jogging together, she looked up to see if his face showed any reaction to her showing up. Pretending that he didn't recognize her, they kept jogging a few minutes together until she asked if they could stop as she'd like to talk to him.

"OK, let's stop at the picnic table," came his response. Once at the table, after a closer look he recognize her; Sarah took out the ribbons and asked, "Do these ribbons look familiar to you?"

"They look like mine."

"I found them in my car, and I don't know how they got there," Sarah explained.

"I had no idea I lost them. Do you work around here?"

"I'm a singer working down at the Sandy Hook Restaurant."

"Well there. My friends and I have been down there. Maybe, I dropped them on the floor, and your shoe picked them up, or they got caught on your clothing and they fell off on the car floor."

With that John yelled, "Wolfie, we have to get back!"

"I'll be right there." Then I turned to her and said, "Wolfie, that's my name."

"My name is Sarah," she introduced herself.

"Well, Sarah, if you want to continue this conversation, we could meet at the Outpost Bar at about 6."

Sarah smiled, "OK. I'll drop by and see if you're there."

While jogging back to the barracks, Wayne asked, "Who is that?"

"She is the singer at the Sandy Hook Restaurant. The one we watch from the hill," I replied as we headed back into the barracks.

CHAPTER 52

That evening only two ships came in, and our team was not scheduled to load, so we headed down to the Outpost at around 6 p.m. It was a real cool evening, so we were sitting outside looking at the river when Sarah and her friend came up to the table and said, "Hello."

We are all stood up. "Hello," I replied and introduced Wayne, Freddie, and Charlie. "And as you know, my name is Wolfie."

Sarah introduced her girlfriend Rose and sat down. We started to talk about everything in general, laughing at some clean jokes while drinking beer and listening to the music. Sarah asked me to dance with her, and as we were slowly dancing, Sarah asked, "Where do you come from?"

I replied, "Long Island!"

"No. I mean where did you grow up?"

I replied, "O-Zone Park, Richmond Hill."

"What a coincidence. We grew up there, too," replied Sarah. "I was talking to my older sister about the weird incident I had, and I mentioned your name. She said that she remembers a guy with your name helping her. And she told me an interesting story.

"My sister was about 19 and hung around a rough crowd. She met a guy in a bar and was having a ball with him when he got drunk and started to beat on her. Nobody helped her; then out of nowhere, a tall, slim, good-looking guy came over and ripped the bully off her. He beat the living shit out of him, then he picked her up, walked over to two girls sitting at a table, and told them to take her in the bathroom and help her refresh herself. When she came out, he was gone. She asked around and was told his name was Wolfie. All she remembers is he had a scar on the side of his head above the eyebrow and a nice smile."

As she slipped the ribbons into my pocket, Sarah continued, "Sounds a lot like you."

I replied, "It might have been. And if it were, it had to have been a very long time ago." With that the music stopped. We walked over to the table. I said, "Well, everybody, looks like I am the only married one, so I'll leave you guys."

Wayne asked, "How are you going to get back?"

"Cab! Good night, everybody!" Then I left.

The weeks flew by, and Sarah and her girlfriend got to know the rest of the teams. When we had nothing to do, we would go up to the hill and watch Sarah and her friends practice during the day and perform at night.

CHAPTER 53

Finally, one day the chief came in and said, "Everybody pack your bags. We're going back to Governors Island. It's over for us. We leave tomorrow."

That night we all went to the Outpost to celebrate. Even the senior chief came. It was a good time for all and a night to remember. The following morning, we got up, had breakfast, got into our black Suburbans, and headed out. We stopped at the hill to see if Sarah was practicing and saw her singing on the stage. We beeped the horn; she waved back to us, and one by one our Suburbans pulled away and headed back toward Governors Island.

Once we reached Governors Island, we were told to put our sea bags in our cars and report to the church at 1300 (or 1:00 p.m.). We were waiting there when the commander approached the platform and said, "As a grateful nation, we thank you for your sacrifice and service. You are hereby dismissed from active duty. Good luck."

The senior chief said, "All of you can pick up your DD 214 forms at the admin office." Then he continued, "Will Petty Officer Wolfinger please report to me now?"

I walked over to the senior chief and the commander who was standing next to him. "Here is your DD 214. You deserve the Purple Heart for the wounds you received. Unfortunately, because it's classified, it will be on your DD 214, but your name will not be on the medal."

"Thank you, Commander. Thank you, Senior Chief." I saluted then left.

Even though it was a long ride home, time went fast as I was thinking about everything I did in the past, and seeing my Judy again. I arrived at home about 3 in the afternoon. When I walked in the door, Judy was in the kitchen cooking. She turned around when she heard the door open. When she saw me, she started to cry and hug me and kiss me, and then she grabbed my hand and said, "Let's go, the kids are not home."

Like teenagers, laughing and giggling, we ran upstairs to our bedroom. We undressed quickly, eager to release our desire for each other. It felt so good to feel her soft body against mine, to smell her perfume, and to touch the softness of her hair. Our lovemaking was fierce and passionate.

After our lovemaking, we lay in each other's arms as sweat rolled off of our bodies, contented and happy that the nightmare was over. After a while, we heard the kids come in, yelling, "Dad." So, I quickly dressed and met them at the head of steps as they came running up. They kept saying they missed me, and I reassured them that I missed them. That night we all went out to dinner to celebrate.

The next day Judy told me that a Dr. Ambrosia called and said that I should come to his office for a physical on Wednesday at 10:00 a.m., so he could approve me to go back to work.

CHAPTER 54

Wednesday at 10:00 a.m. I was sitting in the waiting room when a nurse came out and said that I should follow her. I followed her to a room, and when we arrived, she said, "Please go in and wait for the doctor. He will be with you shortly."

I entered the room to find a spread of Italian food laid out on the exam table. I heard the adjacent door open, and I turned around to see Anthony Zito. We stood looking at each other for a moment; then, we opened up our arms and hugged each other saying, "Blood is blood."

Anthony said, "Thank you, Wolfie. I couldn't depend on anybody but you. Tell me what happened while we share a glass of wine and some good food."

I explained to Anthony that I was taken by surprise when Frank, a truck driver, showed up on my company site right before I was activated for Desert Storm "It had been years since I had last seen him. He pulled me aside to explain to me what had to be done in order to save you. I told him that I owed you my life, and I would do whatever had to be done. I still remember that night when the cops were chasing us, and they caught you, but I kept running."

I continued, "The cop yelled to me, 'Halt or I'll shoot!' And he was about to shoot me in the back, but you screamed, 'Wolfie, he will!' I stopped and turned around with my hands in the air. The cop was so mad, he broke your nose with the gun for yelling to me"

Anthony said, "I remember that night, but you're worth saving. Go on. Continue."

"Frank gave me a burner phone and told me to use it whenever I needed him. Don't know how you got me activated for Desert Storm."

"Everybody has a price. Please continue," Anthony replied

"Everything was going well. Frank told me where and when Sammy the Bull would be jogging with his two FBI agents, the location of the gun, and what to do. I lay in the bushes waiting. As he passed by me, I shot him in his left thigh. He stopped and told the agents, 'Some fucking bug just bit me,' and he kept on running. I lay there for a few minutes until they were out of sight; then I backed out. I took all the stuff and put it into a plastic bag and threw the bag into a garbage pail. I heard the garbage truck coming up the block as I was crossing the street. I turned to see the truck and didn't notice the car coming down the street. The car hit me, breaking a headlight. It turned out not to be anything very serious, but I asked Frankie to have someone change the headlight before the driver woke up and came out to check her car." Once that story was completed, I told Anthony about the run in with Sarah, the ribbons, and Jeff Half.

"While I believe there is nothing to worry about, I recommend burning down Jeff Half's office. He has some pictures of me. I don't think it means anything, but just to be safe, make sure it's accidental."

He held out his hand saying, "Man, it's really great seeing you again, I can't thank you enough Wolfie."

I replied, "Same here, Anthony. It's been years, but it paid off. I remember the day we got out of jail, and I told you that I wasn't coming back. You said that if anybody else said that, they would not be leaving. Any other person would have been taken out. We hugged each other and once again said 'Blood is blood.'"

I left the office, and on the way out, the nurse gave me my papers. I got into my car and started my trip home. While I was driving, my brother called all excited. I said, "So what's up, Charlie?"

"I looked up the family tree. Do you know what our great, great-grand-mother's and father's last name was?"

I replied, "No."

"It was Catherine and Anthony Zito!"

To that, I replied, "Wow!"

Charlie said, "You think we're related to that gangster?"

I replied, "There's a lot of Zitos in this world."

Charlie laughed. "I guess you're right." And we shifted our conversation about family to another topic.

NOTES

The Saints, who had territory near the Queens-Brooklyn border, were in constant clashes with the Brooklyn gangs, among them the Halsey Bops and Tots (an under 18 gang).

There were about 1,000 to 1,500 Saints gang members in all of Queens. Due to their large numbers, the Saints were divided up into divisions with some divisions being so large they had to be divided into even smaller groups labeled "Senior" and "Junior." These divisions were named according to the neighborhood they were from. For example, there were the Woodhaven Saints, Ridgewood Saints, etc.; then depending on the size of each gang, they were separated according to age. For example, the Junior Ridgewood Saints and the Senior Ridgewood Saints.

In 1960, the Junior Saints from Queens had a number of zip guns in their possession and even a rifle. They were enemies with the Halsey Bops and had them in their sights for a big ambush only to have it broken up by the cops.

The 458th deployed to Vietnam in late 1966 as a (LARC-5) Transportation Company to help fulfill the difficult task of helping unload 20.9 million measurement tons of ships' cargo to the beaches of South Vietnam. As the weeks and days went by, two factors developed that changed the 458th from cargo handlers to warriors. As the stockpiles of cargo grew, the resistance from the Viet Cong grew. Beach and ship security had to be improved; 50-caliber machine guns were mounted on a few LACs, and instead of unloading cargo, these LACs started providing waterborne security day and night.